Home Office Research Study 205

Drugs and crime: the results of the second developmental stage of the NEW-ADAM programme

Trevor Bennett
University of Cambridge, Institute of Criminology

Research, Development and Statistics Directorate
Home Office

Home Office Research Studies

The Home Office Research Studies are reports on research undertaken by or on behalf of the Home Office. They cover the range of subjects for which the Home Secretary has responsibility. Titles in the series are listed at the back of this report (copies are available from the address on the back cover). Other publications produced by the Research, Development and Statistics Directorate include Research Findings, the Research Bulletin, Statistical Bulletins and Statistical Papers.

The Research, Development and Statistics Directorate

RDS is part of the Home Office. The Home Office's purpose is to build a safe, just and tolerant society in which the rights and responsibilities of individuals, families and communities are properly balanced and the protection and security of the public are maintained.

RDS is also a part of the Government Statistical Service (GSS). One of the GSS aims is to inform Parliament and the citizen about the state of the nation and provide a window on the work and performance of government, allowing the impact of government policies and actions to be assessed.

Therefore -

Research Development and Statistics Directorate exists to improve policy making, decision taking and practice in support of the Home Office purpose and aims, to provide the public and Parliament with information necessary for informed debate and to publish information for future use.

"The views expressed in this report are those of the authors, not necessarily those of the Home Office (nor do they reflect Government policy)."

First published 2000
Application for reproduction should be made to the Communications and Development Unit, Room 201, Home Office, 50 Queen Anne's Gate, London SW1H 9AT.

© Crown copyright 2000   ISBN 1 84082 498 0
                         ISSN 0072 6435

Foreword

This report gives a clear assessment, underpinned by urine testing, of recent drugs consumption on the part of the general range of suspected offenders arrested by the police. Based on fieldwork in four English locations, it builds on earlier research carried out in five places which was presented in Home Office Research Study 183, Drugs and Crime: the results of research on drug testing and interviewing arrestees (Bennett, 1998).

Two of the five places covered in the present study, Nottingham and Sunderland, were also included in the earlier research. It is therefore possible to discuss changes in drug use by offenders over the period 1997-1999, for these two locations. This type of research has now become a rolling programme, taking in a wider set of places. The programme goes by the acronym NEW-ADAM (New English and Welsh Arrestee Drug Abuse Monitoring). NEW-ADAM will help to track the progress of the Government's drugs strategy.

DAVID MOXON
Head of Crime and Criminal Justice Unit
Research, Development and Statistics Directorate

Acknowledgements

I would like to acknowledge those people who helped in conducting the research. These include:

The Home Office.

The four police forces covered in this report (Metropolitan Police, Merseyside Police, Nottinghamshire Police and Northumbria Police).

The senior officers and custody officers at the four host sites.

The Forensic Science Service at Chepstow.

Stuart Lockhart.

The fieldwork researchers.

The arrestees who were interviewed.

Gail Bennett and Cassandra Bennett.

Staff on the ADAM and I-ADAM programmes at the National Institute of Justice in Washington, D.C.

Trevor Bennett

Contents

Summary

The current report presents the results of four surveys: three conducted as part of the second developmental stage of the NEW-ADAM programme and one conducted as the first survey of the full NEW-ADAM programme. The three second-stage surveys were conducted in London (South Norwood), Liverpool, and Nottingham. The first survey of the NEW-ADAM programme was conducted in Sunderland.

The surveys in South Norwood and Liverpool were selected partly because they were two of the sites used to test the proposed Drug Treatment and Testing Orders. It was hoped that the results of the research would provide some useful additional information which might support the existing evaluations of these schemes. The surveys in Nottingham and Sunderland were selected because they provided an opportunity to conduct repeat surveys in sites already surveyed in the first developmental stage. The findings of the first developmental stage of the research were published in Home Office Research Study 183 (Bennett, 1998).

The main methods of data collection were structured interviews and collection of urine specimens. The research was conducted in police custody suites and was based on samples of arrestees currently held for official processing (typically in relation to a suspected offence).

Urinalysis findings on drug use (Chapter 4)

The urinalysis findings show objectively whether selected drugs had been consumed by arrestees within the last few days. The results presented in the chapter were aggregated to show prevalence rates of positive tests for drug use among different groups of arrestees:

- Sixty-nine per cent of arrestees across the four survey sites tested positive for at least one drug (excluding alcohol). Thirty-six per cent tested positive for multiple (2 or more) drugs (excluding alcohol).

- Twenty-nine per cent of arrestees tested positive for opiates (including heroin) and 20 per cent tested positive for cocaine (including crack).

- Almost half of arrestees (49%) tested positive for cannabis.

- There was a general increase in the prevalence of drug use over the period 1997 to 1999 among arrestees tested in the repeat surveys conducted in Nottingham and Sunderland.

- In both Nottingham and Sunderland, the percentage of arrestees testing positive for cannabis increased (the increase was statistically significant in Sunderland, but not in Nottingham). In both areas the prevalence of positive tests for opiates and cocaine increased (the increases were significant in Nottingham, but just failed to reach significance in Sunderland).

There was some evidence of an escalation of drug use in both areas. However, the pattern of change reflected the different starting points of the two areas. In 1997, arrestees in Nottingham were more heavily involved in 'minor' drugs, whereas arrestees in Sunderland were more heavily involved in alcohol. In 1999, arrestees in Nottingham appeared to escalate from 'minor' to 'major' drugs, whereas arrestees in Sunderland appeared to escalate from alcohol to 'minor' drugs.

(It should be noted that the terms 'major' and 'minor' drugs are used in this report to distinguish heroin and crack/cocaine from other drugs.)

Self-reported drug use (Chapter 5)

There are a number of advantages to asking arrestees to report on their drug misuse. It is possible to examine use over longer periods of time than can be measured using urinalysis. It enables more information to be collected about a wider range of drug types and a wider range of related issues:

- Younger arrestees (aged 17 to 24) were more likely than older arrestees (aged 25 to 59) to have used cannabis and amphetamines in the last 12 months.

- Older arrestees were more likely than younger arrestees to say that they had used heroin and methadone in the last 12 months.

- Older arrestees were also slightly more likely than younger ones to report using powder cocaine or crack in the last 12 months (although the difference was not statistically significant).

- There was some variation across the four locations in patterns of drug misuse. The highest rates of cocaine and heroin use were in Liverpool. The highest prevalence rates of amphetamine use in the last 12 months were in Sunderland. The prevalence of cannabis use was fairly even across the research sites.

- There was some evidence of an increase in crack use and heroin use in both Nottingham and Sunderland over the period 1997 to 1999. There was also evidence of a reduction in the use of ecstasy and LSD across the two sites.

The self-report results confirm the urinalysis results which suggest that there has been an increase in the prevalence of the use of heroin and crack over the last two years, and in some of the survey sites (most notably Liverpool) the recent prevalence of use of these drugs is particularly high.

Expenditure on drugs (Chapter 6)

The amount spent on drugs provides another indicator of the prevalence of drug misuse among arrestees. However, expenditure on drugs can also indicate the regularity of use of drugs and the frequency of involvement in the process of seeking and purchasing drugs:

- The average weekly expenditure on drugs, among all arrestees who had consumed at least one illegal drug in the last 12 months, was £129. The highest weekly expenditure was in Liverpool (an average of £192 per week) and the lowest was in Sunderland (an average of £72 per week).

- Younger arrestees (aged under 25) tended to report lower levels of expenditure than older arrestees (aged 25 to 59).

- Arrestees who used both heroin and crack/cocaine in the last 12 months reported the highest levels of expenditure (their average expenditure in the last seven days was £308).

● Users of heroin and crack/cocaine constituted 30 per cent of arrestees who used one or more drugs in the last 12 months and were responsible for over 70 per cent of the total expenditure on drugs.

● Mean expenditure on drugs among users of both heroin and crack/cocaine increased slightly in Nottingham over the period 1997 to 1999 and decreased slightly in Sunderland. In neither area was the change statistically significant.

On average, users of both heroin and crack/cocaine spent over £16,000 a year on drugs and in some locations this average was closer to £20,000. The average amounts spent per user did not change substantially from 1997 to 1999, suggesting that the combination of the price of these drugs and the amount consumed had more or less remained constant over this period of time.

Illegal income (Chapter 7)

The chapter on illegal income is the first of three chapters that aims to investigate the links between drug use and crime. Illegal income is a broader concept than acquisitive crime or property crime. It covers a variety of ways in which arrestees might obtain income in cash or in kind in addition to the normal legal routes of employment or state benefits:

● On average, arrestees reported generating just over £5,000 in illegal income in the last year. This amount varied slightly by area, with arrestees in Liverpool reporting the highest rates (an average of about £9,000 in the last year) and arrestees in Sunderland reporting the lowest rates (an average of about £2,000 in the last year).

● The highest levels of illegal income were reported by those who used both heroin and crack/cocaine, who had mean illegal incomes of almost £13,000 in the last year.

● The heroin and crack/cocaine-using group comprised 23 per cent of the total number of arrestees, yet generated 52 per cent of the total illegal income.

● Heroin and crack/cocaine users generated a combined total illegal income in the last 12 months of just over £2 million.

The chapter concluded by estimating the amount of illegal income that might be connected to heroin and crack/cocaine use. If heroin and crack/cocaine users had the same illegal incomes as the non-heroin and crack/cocaine users, it was estimated that the combined total illegal income of all arrestees would have been 52 per cent lower.

Self-reported crime (Chapter 8)

Arrestees were also asked about their involvement in property crime. There is a difference between commission of common types of property crime and generation of illegal income (discussed above). Illegal income might not derive from property crime and property crime might not generate illegal income (especially if the offender is unsuccessful). The main reason for including separate questions on property crime is to identify which crime types arrestees most frequently commit and to determine the connection between the commission of these crime types and drug misuse:

- Just over one-quarter (28%) of arrestees said that they had stolen from a shop and a similar percentage (27%) said that they had handled stolen goods in the last 12 months. Fewer arrestees said that they had committed robbery or had stolen items from the person (e.g. bag snatches).

- Users of both heroin and cocaine were more than five times more likely to report committing robbery and more than four times more likely to report shoplifting than arrestees who did not use these drugs. They were also three times more likely to report residential and non-residential burglary.

- Over two-thirds of the highest-rate offenders (20 offences a month or more) reported using heroin or crack/cocaine.

- Nine per cent of the total sample of arrestees could be classified as high-rate offenders and users of heroin or crack/cocaine.

- This nine per cent group of high-rate offenders was responsible for one-third (34%) of all illegal income and over one-half (52%) of all reported offences.

Overall, arrestees reported a high number of offences in the last 12 months. The prevalence of shoplifting was particularly high (the majority of arrestees admitted this offence). About one-third of all arrestees had committed a vehicle crime and about one-quarter had committed a burglary. There were few clear differences in rate of offending and arrestee characteristics, although younger arrestees tended to report higher rates of offending than older arrestees. The clearest difference among arrestees and offending rates occurred in relation to drug use.

Drugs and crime (Chapter 9)

This chapter brings together some of the findings of the previous two chapters and examines the relationship between drugs and crime. The first part of the chapter looks in more detail at the statistical association between measures of drug use and measures of crime. The second part of the chapter considers the causal connection between the two more directly and examines what arrestees say about the link between their own drug use and crime.

- Arrestees who tested positive for three or more drugs reported on average three times as many offences as those who had zero positive tests. They reported committing more than twice as many offence types and eight times the illegal income. They also reported more than twice as many arrests in the last 12 months.

- Arrestees who reported spending £100 or more on drugs reported ten times the number of offences as those who reported no expenditure on drugs. They also reported four times the mean number of offence types committed in the last 12 months, eight times the mean illegal income, and almost twice as many arrests.

- Arrestees who reported using three or more drug types in the last 12 months, reported more offences, more offence types, greater illegal income and more arrests than those who reported using no drug types.

- Just over 40 per cent (42%) of arrestees said that they thought that their drug use and crime were connected.

Overall, the chapter shows that there are a number of strong correlations between certain kinds of drug use and criminal behaviour. While not all of the associations found were statistically significant, the findings in most cases tended to be in the direction of showing that arrestees who used drugs were more likely than those who did not to be involved in criminal behaviour and were also more likely to be more heavily involved in criminal behaviour.

Health and drug dependence (Chapter 10)

One of the many problems associated with drug misuse is drug dependence. In a medical sense, dependence refers to the development of a tolerance for a drug which results in withdrawal symptoms when the drug is removed. In the current chapter, the word 'dependence' is used slightly more broadly to include psychological as well as physical dependence. Specifically, arrestees were asked whether they felt that they needed the drug or felt bad or ill when they did not have it:

- One-third (33%) of arrestees said that they were dependent on at least one prohibited drug at the time of the interview.

- Dependence on heroin was highest in Liverpool (almost one-third of arrestees said that they were currently dependent upon it) and lowest in Sunderland (6% said they were dependent).

- In Nottingham, during the period 1997 to 1999, the percentage of arrestees who said that they were currently dependent on heroin increased from 12 per cent to 23 per cent (statistically significant), whereas the percentage who said that they were currently dependent on alcohol decreased (also significant).

- In Sunderland, there was an increase in the percentage of arrestees who said that they were dependent on heroin. However, this relationship was not statistically significant. There was also a notable reduction in the percentage of arrestees who said that they were dependent on alcohol, which was statistically significant.

- Just over one per cent of all arrestees thought that they were HIV positive (1% among heroin and/or crack/cocaine users) and about seven per cent said that they mixed with people who were HIV positive (12% among heroin and/or crack/cocaine users).

- One per cent of the sample said that they currently had hepatitis (2% among heroin and/or crack/cocaine users) and about eight per cent said that they mixed with people who had hepatitis (17% among heroin and/or crack/cocaine users).

Arrestees experienced various kinds of health problems. In addition to drug dependence, a sizeable minority was currently under prescription from a doctor or had recently purchased drugs over-the-counter for a range of illnesses. Almost one-fifth of arrestees currently receiving prescribed drugs were suffering from depression (18%). A further five per cent of arrestees under prescription were suffering from anxiety attacks. Other common health problems included back pain (6% of those receiving a prescription) and asthma (experienced by 11% of arrestees currently on a prescription).

Injecting behaviour (Chapter 11)

Injection is potentially the most harmful way of administering drugs. It carries various kinds of health risk to the user (such as infection, abscesses and the risk of overdose) and various kinds of health risk to others (such as cross infection when equipment is shared and health problems relating to disposal of used syringes):

- About one-quarter (23%) of arrestees said that they had injected an illegal drug at some time in their lives and about one-fifth (20%) said that they had done so in the last 12 months.

- The most frequently injected drug in the last 12 months was heroin (14% of arrestees had injected it) followed by cocaine (8%) and amphetamines (8%).

- The incidence of injection was highest among heroin users, who injected on average 20 days out of the last 30 days. Methadone and cocaine injectors did so on average just under once every other day (14 days out of the last 30). Injectors of amphetamines and other drugs did so at the lower rate of 12 days and 10 days out of the last 30 days respectively.

- The prevalence of injection of any drug increased in both Nottingham and Sunderland over the period 1997 to 1999.

- Six per cent of all arrestees interviewed said that they had shared a needle at some time in their lives and four per cent said that they had done so in the last 12 months.

A sizeable minority of all 'major' users injects the drugs and a sizeable minority of these shares their needles. There is some evidence from the Nottingham and Sunderland surveys that the prevalence of injection might be increasing in line with the general increase in prevalence of heroin and crack/cocaine use among arrestees.

Treatment (Chapter 12)

The extent of the unmet need for treatment among drug users is unknown. In the current surveys, arrestees were asked whether they had ever been in treatment and whether they currently wanted treatment:

- About one-fifth (21%) of all arrestees had received treatment for drug misuse at some time in their lives and just over one-quarter (29%) said that they currently had a need for treatment.

- Of those who said that they currently needed treatment, about one-third of them (9% of the total sample) said that they were receiving treatment and two-thirds of them (20% of the total sample) said that they were not currently receiving treatment.

- There was little change over the period 1997 to 1999 in the use of treatment facilities among arrestees in Nottingham and Sunderland.

- Four per cent of arrestees in Sunderland who were arrested locally (within 5 miles from the current custody suite) and three per cent of those arrested out of the local area had received help or information about drugs while in police custody.

- In most cases, the help or information was individual counselling or information leaflets. In most cases, the help or information offered was not followed up.

The results suggest that there is a substantial unmet need for treatment services among drug-misusing arrestees. Their treatment needs are fairly mixed, combining programmes that will get them off drugs with programmes that will make their drug misuse safer and better controlled. At the time of the current surveys, there were few arrest referral schemes in operation and only limited help or advice was offered to arrestees while in police custody, in addition to that provided within requirements of the Police and Criminal Evidence Act 1984.

Drug markets (Chapter 13)

One of the important factor that affects the level of drug use is local availability. If there are few drugs available in a local area, then at least some of the potential purchasers of these drugs will be unable to obtain them. The same argument applies to the ease of making the purchase. If it is difficult to make a purchase locally, because the drugs are sold through fairly inaccessible closed markets, then some of the potential purchasers of these drugs will be unable to obtain them.

- At the time of the survey, over 80 per cent of arrestees were able to obtain either crack/cocaine (82%) or heroin (85%) in their local neighbourhood. In other words, it was not necessary for them to travel beyond their local neighbourhood to obtain their drugs.

- The average number of dealers known to arrestees was 12 in relation to crack/cocaine and 15 in relation to heroin.

- In Nottingham, 50 per cent of arrestees in 1997 said that they could buy crack/cocaine in their own neighbourhood and 60 per cent said that they could buy heroin in their own neighbourhood. In 1999, 81 per cent of arrestees said that they could buy crack/cocaine locally and 83 per cent said that they could buy heroin locally. Both increases were statistically significant.

- In Nottingham, the mean number of people from whom arrestees could buy crack/cocaine increased from 10.3 in 1997 to 13.4 in 1999. Similarly, the number of people from whom arrestees could buy heroin increased from 13.8 in 1997 to 18.5 in 1999. However, neither change was statistically significant.

- In Sunderland, there was no evidence of a change in availability of drugs during the period 1997 to 1999.

The changes in availability of drugs (as measured through the ability to make local purchases) and the number of dealers known to the user to some extent mirror the changes in the pattern of drug use in the two areas. In Nottingham, there was a significant increase across the two surveys in the proportion of arrestees involved in crack/cocaine and heroin, whereas, in Sunderland, there was less evidence of an increase in the use of these drugs among arrestees.

Weapons and guns (Chapter 14)

The possession and ownership of weapons and guns is problematic in a general sense, and legislation has recently been passed to tackle this problem by controlling the spread of both legal and illegal firearm possession. The use of weapons and guns in relation to drug use and drug purchases is especially problematic as it increases the harm associated with drug use to include the possibility of injury or death:

- About a quarter of arrestees (27%) said that they had carried a weapon (other than a gun) at the time of an offence at some time in their lives. Fifteen per cent said that they had carried a weapon at the time of an offence in the last 12 months.

- About one-third (36%) of arrestees said that they had owned or had easy access to a gun at some time in their lives and about one-quarter (24%) said that they had done so in the last 12 months.

- In Nottingham, there was a small (non-significant) increase in gun ownership and access during the period 1997 to 1999 (increasing from 16% to 20%). There was no change in the proportion of arrestees who said that they mixed with people who owned or had easy access to guns.

- In Sunderland, there was also a small and non-significant increase in gun ownership and easy access (23% to 27%), which was accompanied by a small reduction in the number of people mixed with who owned or had easy access to a gun.

The chapter shows what might be regarded as high levels of involvement of arrestees with guns and other weapons. There is some indication (not statistically significant) that gun ownership and easy access to guns may have increased slightly since 1997.

Conclusion (Chapter 15)

The final chapter discusses the context of the NEW-ADAM programme and the current state of knowledge about patterns and trends in drug misuse. It summarises the results of recent research and discusses what has been learned from the ADAM programme in the United States and the I-ADAM research consortium. The chapter concludes by describing the plan of action of the NEW-ADAM programme over the next few years.

1   The NEW-ADAM programme

In 1999, the government allocated £6 million of new money for research and information gathering in support of the government's drugs strategy. Part of the £6 million was used to set up a national programme of research on interviewing and voluntary drug testing of arrestees. The programme was formally established in July 1999 under the title of the New English and Welsh Arrestee Drug Abuse Monitoring Programme (NEW-ADAM). It is currently managed by the Home Office Research, Development and Statistics Directorate and conducted by the University of Cambridge.

Before the establishment of the national programme, there were two stages of developmental research. The results of the first stage were published in 1998 in a Home Office Research Studies report (Bennett, 1998). The results of the second stage are contained in this current report.

Government policy

The national programme of research and the earlier developmental stages of the research have been closely linked to government policy on drugs. In 1994, the previous government issued a White Paper called, 'Tackling Drugs Together: A Consultation Document on a Strategy for England 1995-1998'. The Paper noted that there was no reliable statistical measure of the amount of drug-related crime. It identified the need to reduce drug-related crime as one of the key aims of the strategy and proposed the development of new ways of measuring the impact of drug misuse on crime as a means of evaluating progress.

In April 1998, the current government published a parliamentary paper called, 'Tackling Drugs to Build a Better Britain: The Government's 10-Year Strategy for Tackling Drug Misuse', based on a report by the UK Anti-Drugs Co-ordinator (HMG, 1998). The publication identified four main elements of the strategy: (1) to help young people resist drug misuse, (2) to protect communities from drug-related, antisocial and criminal behaviour, (3) to enable people with drug problems to overcome them, and (4) to stifle the availability of illegal drugs on the streets.

The first annual report of the UK Anti-Drugs Co-ordinator, published in 1999, elaborated on the main objectives of the policy and the key targets relating to them. Key Objective 1 aims to reduce drug use generally and drug use among young people in particular. The key performance target relating to this objective is to reduce the proportion of people under 25 reporting use of illegal drugs in the last month and previous year. Specifically, it aims to reduce the proportion of young people using the drugs which cause the greatest harm (heroin and cocaine) by 50 per cent by 2008 and by 25 per cent by 2005. Other targets include delaying the age of onset of use of Class A drugs by 6 months and reducing by 20 per cent the numbers of 11-to-16-year-olds who use Class A drugs.

Key Objective 2 aims to break the links between drugs and crime and reduce the levels of repeat offending among drug misusing offenders. In particular, it aims to reduce levels of repeat offending amongst drug misusing offenders by 50 per cent by 2008 and 25 per cent by 2005. Other targets include reducing the proportion of arrestees who test positive for Class A drugs.

Key Objective 3 aims to increase the participation of problem drug misusers, including prisoners, in drug treatment programmes which have a positive impact on health and crime by 100 per cent by 2008 and by 66 per cent by 2005. The report also aims to reduce the number of users in treatment who report injecting drugs and to reduce the number of those injecting who report sharing their equipment. Other objectives include reducing the incidence of Hepatitis B and encouraging local Drug Action Teams (DATs) to generate local action plans to tackle drug misuse.

Key Objective 4 aims to stifle the availability of illegal drugs on the streets. In particular, it aims to reduce access to all drugs amongst young people (aged under 25) and to reduce access to drugs which cause the greatest harm, particularly heroin and cocaine, by 50 per cent by 2008 and 25 per cent by 2005. Other aims include increasing the percentage of heroin and cocaine seized which was destined for Europe and the UK.

The developmental research

In 1995, the Home Office funded a small feasibility study to determine whether it would be possible and useful to interview and collect voluntary urine specimens from arrestees. The aim of the research was to examine methods of determining drug use prevalence among offenders and to understand more fully the links between drug misuse and crime. The report of the study reviewed the literature on a similar programme of interviewing and drug testing in the United States and concluded that it was possible and urged the development of a similar programme in England and Wales (Bennett, 1995).

In the same year, the Home Office commissioned the first stage of developmental research. The research was conducted in five police areas in England and Wales over 18 months during 1996 and 1997. The results of the research were published in 1998 (Bennett, 1998).

In 1998, a second developmental stage of research was commissioned by the Home Office with the aim of building upon the earlier developmental research and moving closer towards a research design that might be used as a basis for a national programme. The research was based in three police force areas and included two new sites and one repeat site surveyed previously in the first developmental stage. The aim of including a repeat site was to test out some of the principles involved in measuring trends in drug misuse among arrestees over time. The results of the second developmental stage are published in this report, together with those from Sunderland (the first location in the NEW-ADAM programme).

The ADAM programme in the United States

The NEW-ADAM programme (including the research conducted during the second developmental stage) is based on a programme of research first conducted in the United States. Since the late 1980s, the United States has operated a large research programme based on interviewing and drug-testing samples of arrestees. The programme was originally called the Drug Use Forecasting Programme (DUF) and more recently has been re-launched as the Arrestee Drug Abuse Monitoring Programme (ADAM). The programme currently covers 35 sites and it is planned to expand to 75 or more sites in the next few years. The main aim of the programme is to identify trends in drug use among arrestees.

The I-ADAM programme

The NEW-ADAM programme is also linked to the I-ADAM (International-Arrestee Drug Abuse Monitoring) programme. The I-ADAM programme comprises a partnership of countries involved in conducting research on interviewing and drug-testing arrestees. The programme is modelled on the US ADAM programme.

I-ADAM was launched in 1998 at an international conference in Miami attended by representatives of eight countries including: Australia, Chile, England, The Netherlands, Panama, Scotland, South Africa and Uruguay. At the time of writing, ADAM-type programmes have been tested and/or established in eight countries (Australia, Chile, England, Malaysia, The Netherlands, Scotland, South Africa and Taiwan).

The main aim of I-ADAM is to generate standardised data on drug use among arrestees in order to compare patterns and trends in drug use over time. It also aims to provide an international research base for co-ordinating drug research and drug control policies. NIJ provides technical assistance to I--ADAM countries in initiating and operating the programme. A web page for the I-ADAM programme has also been created and can be accessed on http://www.adam-nij.net/adam/iadam.htm.

The NEW-ADAM programme

The NEW-ADAM programme was launched in July 1999 and was funded to run for three years in the first instance. The programme is based on financial years, with the first year (a shorter year) running from July 1999 to March 2000. The second year will run from April 2000 to March 2001 and the third year will run from April 2001 to March 2002. In each financial year, eight surveys will be conducted in police force areas in England and Wales. In Year 1, eight surveys (at the time of writing) have been completed. In Year 2, eight additional sites will be selected and surveyed. In Year 3, the first eight sites will be revisited for the first round of repeat surveys. Subject to funding, in Year 4, the second eight sites will be revisited for the second round of repeat surveys. Hence, the core NEW-ADAM programme will comprise a rolling programme of research based on 16 locations, surveyed at two-yearly intervals. A force report is produced for each survey at each location and is made available to the local police. An annual report containing the findings of the previous year (plus any trend analyses relating to earlier years) will be more widely published.

Aims of the second developmental stage

In general, the aim of the research was to continue to develop procedures for drug testing and interviewing arrestees that might form the basis of a national programme of drug testing, should funds become available. Specifically, the aims were:

- to develop further the procedures for interviewing and voluntary drug testing of arrestees

- to measure prevalence and change in drug misuse among representative samples of arrestees in selected police force areas

- to measure prevalence and change in expenditure on drugs

- to measure prevalence and change of income-generating crime among arrestees and to investigate links between drug misuse and crime

- to measure prevalence and change in self-reported offending

- to identify health and lifestyle problems relating to drug misuse

- to determine the level of treatment received and help offered to solve drug-related problems

- to investigate any other problems and issues relating to arrestees that are deemed to be of current interest or concern.

The research surveys and locations

The current report is based on the results of the three surveys conducted in the second developmental stage and the first survey of the NEW-ADAM programme. The three second stage surveys were conducted in South Norwood (August 1998 – Metropolitan Police District), Liverpool (September 1998 – Merseyside Police), and Nottingham (January 1999 – Nottinghamshire Police). The first survey of the NEW-ADAM programme was conducted in Sunderland (July 1999 – Northumbria Police). The surveys in South Norwood and Liverpool were selected partly because they were two of the sites used for the initial piloting of Drug Treatment and Testing Orders. It was hoped that the results of the research would provide some useful additions to the existing evaluations of these schemes. Nottingham and Sunderland were selected because they provided an opportunity to conduct repeat surveys in sites already surveyed in the first developmental stage.

The scope and structure of the report

It should be emphasised that the following analysis and discussion are based on the findings of the developmental stage of the NEW-ADAM programme. The programme and the methods (as the title suggests) were still under development. Some of the research problems identified during this stage (notably the specimen collection rates and some aspects of the question phrasing) have since been addressed. However, the developmental stage surveys were conducted using sound sampling and research methods and (despite some later improvements) were sufficiently robust to provide valid estimates of prevalence and trends in drug misuse among arrestees.

The current report summarises the main findings of this research. The report opens with an introduction which gives an overview to the research and briefly describes the research methods. It is then divided into four main parts which address the four main aims of the government's drug policy: to reduce drug use among young people, to reduce drug-related crime, to increase the use of treatment facilities and to reduce the availability of illegal drugs.

The introductory chapters discuss the context of the research.

- *The NEW-ADAM programme:* this chapter introduces key features of the NEW-ADAM programme, provides an overview of the second developmental stage of the research, discusses the policy context of the research and identifies the survey dates and locations.

- *Research methods:* this chapter outlines the methods used for collecting the interview data and collecting and transporting the urine specimens.

- *Achieved samples:* the chapter on sampling discusses the method of selecting arrestees for interview and investigates the difference between the sample and the population.

Part One examines the prevalence and nature of drug use among arrestees and looks at changes over time. Brief comparisons are made with the general population:

- *Urinalysis findings on drug use:* this chapter presents the findings relating to the prevalence of positive tests for various kinds of drugs from the results of the urinalysis.

- *Self-reported drug use:* this discusses arrestees' admitted drug use over various periods of time, including in the last 12 months, the last month and in the last three days for 19 different drug types.

- *Expenditure on drugs:* the amount spent on drugs over the last seven days and over the last year is summarised and compared for different demographic groups and different types of drug user.

Part Two looks at self-reported offending among arrestees and the relationship between drug use and crime:

- *Illegal income:* the amount of illegal income generated over the last 12 months is compared for different demographic groups and different types of drug user.

- *Self-reported crime:* this chapter reports the findings of self-reported offending among arrestees in relation to ten common income-generating crimes.

- *Drugs and crime:* various measures of drug use and crime are correlated and arrestees' views on the connection between their own drug use and crime are presented.

Part Three considers health issues relating to drug dependence, injecting drugs, sharing needles and arrestees' experience of treatment.

- *Drug dependence*: the prevalence of dependence on different types of drugs is presented.

- *Injecting behaviour:* this chapter examines the prevalence of injection drugs.

- *Treatment*: arrestees' previous experience of treatment services and their current treatment needs are discussed.

Part Four looks at the availability of the most addictive drugs (heroin and crack/cocaine) on the streets and the way in which arrestees obtain their drugs:

- *Drug markets:* this chapter examines the way in which users of heroin and crack/cocaine purchase their drugs and the ease with which they are able to obtain drugs.

- *Weapons and guns:* this chapter investigates the use of weapons and guns in crime and discusses arrestees' reasons for possessing or having access to a gun.

The final chapter concludes by considering the scope of the NEW-ADAM programme in monitoring drug use and in evaluating government policy:

- *Conclusion*: the report concludes by considering what the research tells us about the nature of drug use among offenders and the nature of the problem addressed by current drugs strategy. The report ends by considering the extent to which data from the NEW-ADAM programme can provide an effective tool for monitoring changes in drug misuse over time and for evaluating the effectiveness of drug-prevention policy.

2   Research methods

The main methods of data collection were structured interviews and collection of urine specimens. The research was conducted in police custody suites and was based on samples of arrestees currently held for official processing (typically in relation to a suspected offence). The research methods adopted were similar to those used in the Arrestee Drug Abuse Monitoring (ADAM) programme in the United States.

The surveys covered in this report were conducted during the period August 1997 to July 1999 in South Norwood in the Metropolitan Police District, Copy Lane in Liverpool, Nottingham Central in Nottingham and Sunderland City in Sunderland. The surveys each took about 30 days to complete, during which time at least one interviewer was present in the police custody block 24 hours a day and seven days a week.

Sampling

The main aim was to generate a probability sample of arrestees. In order to obtain a sufficient number of interviews over the time available, it was necessary to attempt to generate a 100 per cent sample. In practice, it was necessary to exclude certain groups of arrestees as ineligible.

The main grounds for exclusion were: if arrestees were unfit for interview, if they were unable to understand what was said during the interview, if they were unsafe to interview, and if they were unsuitable for interview on the grounds of the drug-testing requirements. The main criteria of ineligibility used in the developmental stages of the research were:

Fit for interview

- Arrestees who were persistently unfit due to alcohol intoxication

- Arrestees who were persistently unfit due to drugs intoxication

- Arrestees who were persistently unfit due to ill health or physical condition

Comprehension of interview and informed consent

- Arrestees who were mentally disordered

- Arrestees who would require an interpreter

Potential danger to interviewer

- Arrestees who may be potentially violent

- Arrestees who were deemed ineligible at the discretion of the custody sergeant or gaoler

Drug-testing requirements

- Arrestees who had been in custody in excess of 48 hours

- Prison transfers and arrestees not at liberty prior to entering the custody suite

Other research selection criteria

- Children and juveniles

- Arrestees held only for 'breathtest' or 'drunkenness' offences

- Arrestees previously interviewed

The target sample size for the second developmental stage of the research was within the range 200 to 225 arrestees. The decision to use this particular target range was based on a number of factors: it was the recommended target sample size of the ADAM programme in the United States, it was found to be feasible to interview about this number of arrestees during a one-month survey period, and it was a sufficient number of cases to conduct the statistical analysis.

Urinalysis

In the second developmental stage of the NEW-ADAM programme, seven drug types were tested: cannabinoid metabolite, opiates, methadone, cocaine metabolite, amphetamines, benzodiazepines and alcohol. LSD was included in the first developmental stage, but was dropped in the second developmental stage as no arrestees tested positive. The urinalysis was based on an immunoassay screening test called the Kinetic Interaction of Micro-Particles (KIMS) test.

The cut-off levels used in the developmental stages of the research were generated in collaboration with the Forensic Science Service in order to provide the best balance between over-sensitive and under-sensitive tests. The reason for doing this was to guard against both Type I errors (saying that a test was positive when it was not [i.e. false positives]) and Type II errors (saying that the test was negative when it was not [i.e. false negatives]). The cut-off levels used in the second developmental stage are shown in Table 2.1 below.

Table 2.1: ***Cut-off levels used to determine whether a urine specimen tested positive or negative for selected drug types***

Drug type	Cut-off levels (ngs/ml or mgs/ml)
Alcohol	10
Amphetamines	500
Benzodiazepines	100
Cannabis	50
Cocaine	150
Methadone	300
Opiates	300

Note: Cut-off levels are expressed in nano grams per millilitre, with the exception of alcohol which is expressed as milligrams per 100 millilitres.

The questionnaire

The questionnaire was divided into two main parts: (1) a core questionnaire (which included questions comparable with those used in the ADAM surveys in the United States) and (2) two versions of a follow-up questionnaire containing additional questions on drug use, lifestyle, gun ownership and drug markets. All interviewees completed the core questionnaire, while half the interviewees were randomly allocated to complete either version A or version B of the follow-up questionnaire.

The main schedule was divided into sections covering the principal topic areas of the research, including: self-reported drug use (ever, in the last 12 months, in the last month, and in the last three days); injecting drugs and sharing needles; dependency on drugs and alcohol; drugs and crime; legal and illegal sources of income; amount spent on alcohol and drugs; and treatment needs. The questions were mainly structured with pre-set response categories, although some were open-ended. The main schedule was administered to all arrestees interviewed.

The follow-up schedule was divided into two parts: 'Follow-Up A' covered questions relating to guns and other weapons, and 'Follow-Up B' covered questions relating to drug purchases and drug markets.

Urinalysis versus self-report measures of drug use

There are advantages and disadvantages to both urinalysis and self-report measures of drug use. The main advantage of drug testing based on urinalysis is that it provides a scientifically valid measure of drug use within the known limitations of the test. The main disadvantages of urinalysis (based on screening tests) concern 'specificity' (the ability of the assay to identify a single-chemical component in a mixture of chemicals and biological materials) and 'cross-reactivity' (the ability of a substance other than the drugs in question to produce a positive result). The tests are also limited by the period of detectability of the test. It has been estimated (Wish and Gropper, 1990) that amphetamines are detectable up to 2 days after use; opiates, methadone, cocaine metabolites, and benzodiazepines are detectable up to 3 days, and cannabinoid metabolites are detectable up to 3 days from single use, up to 10 days with daily use, and up to 27 days from chronic use. The main advantage of self-report measures is the ability of the researcher to collect information over a variety of time periods and to cover a wide range of related issues. The main disadvantage of self-report methods is the memory of the respondent and his or her ability to recall drug use over defined times periods. The results are also dependent on the veracity of the respondent and his or her willingness to share this information with the researcher.

The results of research on the validity of urinalysis and self-report measures of drug misuse are fairly mixed. Some writers have argued that self-report measures underestimate drug use when compared with the results of urinalysis (Fendrich and Yanchun, 1994), whereas other writers have argued that urinalysis measures underestimate drug use when compared with the results of self report (Edgar and O'Donnell, 1998). Appendix B of the first report in the current series (Bennett, 1998) compared the self-report and urinalysis findings among arrestees interviewed in the first developmental stage of the research and found that fewer arrestees reported drug use in the last 3 days than tested positive for that drug in relation to each of the drug groups tested. However, there are a number of possible reasons for this disparity.

The NEW-ADAM programme is based on both urine specimen collection and structured interviews. This had been done in order to obtain the advantages of both methods of data collection and to cross check (when appropriate) the results of each.

3

Achieved samples

The aim of the sampling method was to interview all eligible arrestees. In practice, it is seldom (if ever) possible to interview every person selected and some losses will occur. In order to check for differences between the sample and the population, it was necessary to collect information about every arrestee processed within the custody block during the period of the research. This information was then used to identify the nature of the losses and to compare the final achieved sample with the overall population.

Achieved samples

The following table (Table 3.1) summarises the throughput of arrestees during the 30-day period of the research and the number and percentage of arrestees who were approached, interviewed, and provided a urine specimen in the four survey sites. (Details of the 1997 surveys conducted in Nottingham and Sunderland are shown in Appendix B.) The table shows that almost 3,000 arrestees passed through the four custody blocks during the period of the research. About half of these (47%) were eligible to be approached for interview. Two-thirds (65%) of those eligible to be approached were approached and 81 per cent of those approached were eventually interviewed. Overall, 68 per cent of those interviewed provided a urine specimen.

It should be noted that the second developmental stage surveys were (as the name suggests) still under development and the various contact rates mentioned above tended to improve over time. For example, the 'approach rate' for arrestees in South Norwood (the first of the four surveys) was 61 per cent, compared with 85 per cent in Sunderland (the last of the four surveys). Similarly, the 'interview rate' for arrestees in South Norwood was 77 per cent, compared with 84 per cent in Sunderland and the 'specimen rate' was 50 per cent in South Norwood, compared with 93 per cent in Sunderland. However, not all rates improved over time. Table B3.1 in Appendix B presents the comparable contact rates for 1997 and 1999 for Nottingham and Sunderland. The table shows that some rates were higher in the earlier round of surveys than in the more recent round. It is hoped that this volatility in the contact rates will reduce over time as the NEW-ADAM programme becomes more established and its procedures more systematised. There is some evidence of this in the results of the surveys conducted since the start of the main NEW-ADAM programme. At the time of writing (after the first eight surveys), all surveys have achieved specimen collection rates of over 90 per cent and most are close to 95 per cent.

The main reasons given for each of the different kinds of losses are shown in the tables in Appendix A. The main grounds for determining that an arrestee was ineligible were primarily that they were unfit for interview due to alcohol intoxication (29% of all ineligible cases), they were identified as mentally disordered (17%), or they were juveniles (16%)(Table A3.2). The main reasons for not approaching an eligible arrestee were that the arrestee was in custody for a short time only and the interviewer was unable to make contact or had insufficient time to conduct the interview (53%). The next most common reason was that the interviewer was interviewing another arrestee at the time (19%)(Table A3.4). The main reason for not achieving an interview was refusal (62%) (Table A3.6) and the main reasons for not achieving a urine specimen were refusal (34%) and inability to provide a specimen after having agreed to do so (30%) (Table A3.8).

Table 3.1: Achieved samples in the four survey areas

	South Norwood		Liverpool		Nottingham		Sunderland		Total	
	n	% of previous row	n	% of previous row	n	% of previous row	n	% of previous row	n	% of previous row
Total arrestees processed	569	100	839	100	909	100	654	100	2,971	100
Arrestees eligible	311	55	415	49	420	46	255	39	1,401	47
Arrestees approached[1]	189	61	262	63	244	58	216	85	911	65
Arrestees interviewed[2]	145	77	209	80	204	84	182	84	740	81
Arrestees providing a urine specimen[3]	73	50	132	63	132	65	169	93	506	68

Notes: [1][2][3] These percentages are sometimes referred to in the text as 'approach rate', 'interview rate', and 'specimen rate' respectively.

Characteristics of the sample and populations

It is not necessarily the case that attrition in the sampling process results in an unrepresentative sample. It is possible that the losses did not follow any particular pattern (such as males being less likely to co-operate than females or younger arrestees less likely than older arrestees).

In order to determine the representativeness of the sample, it is necessary to compare the achieved sample with the eligible population. However, it is worth pointing out that there were slight differences between the two groups which might affect the comparison. It was mentioned earlier that the sample of eligible arrestees excluded those who had already been interviewed during the survey period (even if they had been re-arrested for a new offence). However, the population of arrestees included a small number of 'repeat' arrestees held on more than one occasion during the survey period.

Hence, the sample comprised unique arrestees, whereas the population comprises unique 'arrest events'. In order to compare like with like, it would be necessary either: (1) to exclude repeat arrestees from the population and from the sample, or (2) to include repeat arrestees in the population and the sample. It is not practically possible to satisfy either of these options in relation to the second-developmental stage research.

This problem has since been resolved in the current NEW-ADAM surveys by using an anonymous marker to identify each unique individual in the population. However, for the time being, the comparison has to be made of the arrest events recorded in the population with the unique arrestees recorded in the sample. In practice, this only makes a marginal difference to the results.

The characteristics of the sample and the population are compared in Table 3.2. This has been done in relation to sex, age and race for all four survey sites. The table shows that the various samples and populations are very similar. The proportion of males and females in the samples are within a few percentage points of the proportion in the populations. However, in both South Norwood and Nottingham males were slightly over-represented in the sample. The proportion of arrestees aged under 25 in the four samples was within two or three percentage points of the population in all surveys. Similarly, in most cases, the proportion of arrestees identified as non-white in the samples was within a few percentage points of the population. The largest difference was in Nottingham where non-whites were slightly under-represented in the sample.

Table 3.2: *Characteristics of the eligible population and achieved interview sample in the four survey areas*

Percentages

		South Norwood		Liverpool		Nottingham		Sunderland	
		Sample	Pop-ulation	Sample	Pop-ulation	Sample	Pop-ulation	Sample	Pop-ulation
		n=145	n=311	n=209	n=415	n=204	n=420	n=182	n=255
Sex	Male	94	88	87	87	83	77	86	85
	Female	6	12	13	13	17	23	14	15
	Total	100	100	100	100	100	100	100	100
Age	17–19	20	21	16	21	24	22	29	27
	20–24	19	16	28	26	31	30	20	20
	25–29	25	24	20	18	20	21	18	18
	30–59	35	38	36	35	25	26	34	35
	60 or over	1	1	0	1	0	1	0	1
	Total	100	100	100	101	100	100	101	101
Race	White	61	59	99	99	85	81	98	98
	Non-white	39	41	1	1	15	19	2	2
	Total	100	100	100	100	100	100	100	100

Notes: The population includes eligible cases only. Percentages calculated on valid cases only. It should be noted that the sample is based on unique arrestees (repeat arrestees are not included), whereas the population is based on arrest events (repeat arrestees are included). The table does not include significance tests as the comparison groups are not based on independent samples. In more recent surveys, it has been possible to identify repeat arrestees in the population and to calculate the characteristics of the sample and the population on the basis of unique individuals.

Conclusion

The method of sampling and the procedures adopted for selecting and interviewing arrestees were under development at the time of the second stage of the research, and many of the problems identified have since been corrected in the first few NEW-ADAM programme surveys. It is hoped to move even closer towards the 'approach rates', 'interview rates' and 'specimen collection rates' that are achieved in the US ADAM programme. This has already been achieved in the initial surveys of the NEW-ADAM programme in relation to specimen rates, which to date range from 90 per cent to 98 per cent of all arrestees interviewed. Improvements in approach rates and interview rates are also being made. Similarly, the more recent methods adopted in the NEW-ADAM programme for identifying 'repeat' arrestees will allow more effective comparisons in the future of the sample and population data.

Part One: Drug misuse among arrestees

Key Performance Target One

The first key performance target of the current drugs strategy is to reduce the proportion of people aged under 25 reporting use of illegal drugs in the last month and previous year substantially, and to reduce the proportion of young people using the drugs which cause the greatest harm – heroin and cocaine – by 50 per cent by 2008 and by 25 per cent by 2005. In addition, the strategy aims to delay the age of first use of Class A drugs (including heroin and crack/cocaine) by six months by 2002.

Monitoring drug misuse

A key element of the government's drugs strategy is assessing effectiveness by monitoring patterns and trends in drug use over time. This is to be achieved by a range of new data collection methods (including the NEW-ADAM programme). However, there already exists a body of research and other information on patterns and trends in drug misuse. These sources can be used in combination with more specialist information to help identify the nature of drug misuse and the success of the policy over time. The major sources of information about drug misuse are commonly divided into social surveys and official statistics (see Parker et al., 1995 for an overview).

Social surveys

The major national, self-report survey of drug misuse is the drugs component of the British Crime Survey (BCS). This component has been included in the last three British Crime Surveys and the results have been published in three Home Office reports (Ramsay and Percy, 1996, Ramsay and Spiller, 1997 and Ramsay and Partridge, 1999). The surveys focus on households and provide information on drug misuse among the general population.

The reports provide a considerable amount of baseline information about the spread of drug misuse across England and Wales and pay particular attention to drug misuse among young people. The results of the most recent survey have shown that about half of young people aged 16 to 19 and a slightly higher percentage of those aged 20 to 24 have used at least one illegal drug at some time in their lives (49% and 55% respectively). However, this rate falls to less than one-third of each group when measuring drug use over the last year (31% and 28% respectively). Cannabis is the most widely-used illegal drug, followed by amphetamines. Consumption of heroin is rare, although six per cent of young people aged 16 to 29 said that they had tried cocaine at some time in their lives.

One of the most important sets of findings of the last survey concerns trends in illegal drug use over the last few years. Over the four-year period from 1994 to 1998, the surveys have shown a significant increase in recent use (in the last 12 months) of cannabis among males (but not females). There has also been a significant increase in recent use of cocaine among all respondents. Most of this increase was a result of changes in use among respondents aged 16 to 29 years and most of this increase occurred across the two most recent surveys (1996 to 1998). There was less evidence of an increase in heroin or heroin substitutes.

Another important national self-report survey is the study conducted by Graham and Bowling (1995), which focused specifically on young people. The survey was based on a random sample of 1,700 young people aged 14 to 25 (plus a booster sample of 800 young people from ethnic minorities). The survey mainly concerned patterns of offending and criminal careers. However, part of the questionnaire examined drug use in the last 12 months.

The study found that drug use in the last year was most prevalent among the 18-to-21-year-olds (47% admitted at least one drug) and least prevalent among the 14-to-17-year-olds (17% admitted at least one drug). It also showed that 29 per cent of males and 15 per cent of all females aged 14 to 25 reported using cannabis in the last year (the most commonly reported drug). This compares with 32 per cent of males and 22 per cent of females aged 16 to 24 (not quite the same age band) who reported recent cannabis use in the 1998 BCS. The slightly higher rates for the BCS might be due to the difference in age of the two groups or difference in the methods used. However, the results are broadly the same and show that a substantial minority of young people has used a least one drug in the recent past.

Another set of important social surveys is the series of surveys of school children conducted by the Schools Health Education Unit in Exeter (see Balding, 1998). The research comprises a number of independent surveys conducted within schools across the country. While they do not constitute a national representative sample, they nevertheless cover a large number of schools and a large number of school children (40,000 in 1999). In the more recent surveys, respondents were questioned about their use of illegal drugs.

The 1997 schools survey showed that nearly three per cent of boys and two per cent of girls aged 11 to 12 had used an illegal drug at some time in their lives (Balding, 1998). The rate of use increased with age with 39 per cent of boys and 40 per cent of girls aged 15 to 16 years reporting using a drug at some time in their lives. The report also summarised the results from preceding surveys and shows an increasing pattern of lifetime drug use among all school children aged 11 to 16 during the period 1987 to 1996. However, in 1997 the prevalence of lifetime drug use declined slightly across nearly all age groups. The most recent report in the series published earlier this year suggests that the decline in lifetime prevalence is continuing among school-aged young people (Balding, 2000).

This trend has also been confirmed in a recent paper by Plant and Miller who found a general reduction in drug use prevalence among 15 and 16 year old students attending state and private schools in the United Kingdom (Plant and Miller, 2000). The reduction applied to all drugs studied, with the exception of heroin use prevalence which increased among both boys and girls.

In addition to the national surveys covering drug misuse, there are a number of local or small-scale surveys which provide information about drug use patterns and trends in drug use in particular locations. The study by Leitner et al. (1993) was based in four cities (3 in England and 1 in Scotland) and comprised a self-report survey of representatives of over 5,000 households. The results of the survey showed drug use in the last 12 months within the main survey sample for all ages (16 years and over) was within the range of five per cent to nine per cent across the four areas. These percentages are lower than those found in the 1994 British Crime Surveys and lower than most of the more recent surveys. The main reasons for the differences may be due to local area variations or the different methods used. It is also possible that the rates are lower because of recent increases in drug use among the general population over time.

One of the most interesting local surveys is the North-West Study. This comprises a longitudinal series of surveys of young people in Liverpool and Manchester (see Parker et al., 1995; Parker et al., 1998 and Brain et al., 1998). The study began in 1991 with a sample of 776 young people selected from eight schools in Merseyside and Greater Manchester. The respondents were subsequently re-interviewed or provided with self-administered questionnaires each year thereafter. The report by Parker et al. (1998) discusses the results of the first five annual sweeps.

The results show what might be regarded as high levels of drug use among these samples of school children. In the 1991 survey, 32 per cent of the 14-year-olds had used cannabis at least once, rising to 59 per cent in the last survey when the respondents were aged 18. Lifetime prevalence of heroin use increased from less than one per cent at age 14 to 6 per cent at age 18 and lifetime prevalence of cocaine use increased from one per cent to six per cent. Unfortunately, it is not possible to untangle the effect of age and the effect of time on the results shown. It is likely that both age and time effects worked together to increase prevalence rates over the course of the five surveys.

Official statistics

The Home Office publishes data on drug seizures and offenders processed through the criminal justice system for drug offences in its statistical bulletin series. Data on drug seizures cover the operations of both the police and HM Customs and Excise and reflect in part organisational activity and in part trends in the importation and distribution of drugs. The reports show that the number of seizures of all drugs, including heroin, cocaine and crack has increased steadily from year to year over the last decade. In 1998, the number of seizures of cannabis increased by seven per cent over the previous year. Cannabis was the most common drug seized and was involved in 76 per cent of seizures. The number of heroin seizures rose by 19 per cent from 1997 to 1998 and the number of crack/cocaine seizures increased by 36 per cent. In 1998, the number of crack seizures was about half the number of cocaine seizures (a proportion which has been declining steadily over the last five years).

Data on offenders processed for drug offences show a similar increasing trend. The number of drug offenders increased by 13 per cent during the period 1997 to 1998. The number of heroin offenders increased by 13 per cent and the number of cocaine offenders processed (excluding crack offenders) increased by 32 per cent (similar percentages to those shown above for changes in the number of seizures). The average age of drug offenders increased slightly from 24.1 in 1993 to just over 25 in 1998. The most notable increases have been among the oldest age group.

Another valuable source of official data on drug misuse is the Department of Health Regional Drug Misuse Databases (RDMDs). The Department of Health publishes regular half-yearly reports in its statistical bulletin series based on the data received from the regional databases (see Department of Health, 1999). The reports provide basic information (individual characteristics and information about the type of drug used) about the number of treatment episodes (the number of times users present to a particular agency) and number of users (unique individuals).

The RDMDs provide useful information on changes in prevalence of the number of people presenting to health agencies for drug-related problems (see Department of Health [1999] for details). During the period March 1994 to March 1999, the number of persons in each six-month period presenting to agencies increased by 60 per cent (from 17,864 to 28,499). During the last full year period of published data (March 1998 to March 1999) the number of persons presenting to health agencies increased by 20 per cent (23,916 to 28,499). In September 1993, the peak age for presenting to treatment was in the age band 25 to 29. Since then the peak age has been in the age band 20 to 24.

In the six-month period ending 31st March 1999, the most commonly recorded drug of misuse was heroin (59% of all users) compared with 56 per cent of all users in the previous six-month period. The second most commonly recorded drug of misuse was methadone (11%), followed by cannabis (10%) and amphetamines (8%). Six per cent of users presenting for treatment were recorded as having cocaine as their main drug of misuse.

Monitoring drug misuse among arrestees

General population surveys and government official statistics tend to paint a similar picture of the current state and recent trends in drug misuse. A number of sources show increasing trends (with the exception of the more recent school surveys) and most show that cannabis and amphetamines are the most common drugs of abuse. The data are also in some agreement in showing that cocaine use is increasing at a slightly higher rate than heroin (albeit from a lower starting point). However, general population surveys and government official statistics do not necessarily cover the entire population of drug users. General population surveys tend to omit difficult-to-reach groups of people, such as homeless people, those currently living in institutions, and those more criminally active (including those who might be imprisoned at the time of the survey). This latter group might also include problematic drug users. Official statistics tend to omit drug users who do not present for treatment (in the case of the RDMDs) or who have not been convicted for a drug offence (in the case of statistics on criminal justice processing).

It is important in assessing the government's drugs strategy that drug misuse monitoring covers a broad spectrum of the population. This should include the difficult-to-reach groups and the more problematic drug users who might not present for treatment or who might not be convicted of a drug offence. The current research aims to shed light on this extreme end of drug users by interviewing and collecting urine specimens from arrestees at their point of contact with the criminal justice system.

The following section comprises three chapters that examine in different ways the prevalence and nature of drug misuse among arrestees. The first examines the results of the urinalysis and the proportion of arrestees who tested positive for different kinds of drugs. The second looks at self-reported drug use and the types of drugs consumed ever and over the last 12 months, the last month, and the last three days. The third examines the amount spent on drugs in the last week and looks at variations in expenditure among different groups.

4   Urinalysis findings on drug use

Information about prevalence of use of various kinds of drugs among different groups can be found in the results of the urinalysis. These results can show scientifically whether selected drugs have been consumed within the last few days. Some drugs, in particular cannabis, have longer half-lives and urinalysis might be able to detect their use up to a period of about one month. As all of the arrestees who provided a urine specimen were interviewed, it is possible to correlate the results of the drug tests with additional information collected on the arrestee.

The following two figures (Figures 4.1 and 4.2) show the percentage of arrestees in each of the four locations who tested positive for each of the seven drug types tested.

The percentage of arrestees who tested positive for any drug (excluding alcohol) ranged from 59 per cent in South Norwood to 77 per cent in Liverpool and the percentage testing positive for multiple drugs (2 or more) ranged from 21 per cent in South Norwood to 55 per cent in Liverpool. The highest rates of positive tests for opiate use (including heroin) were in Liverpool (exactly half of all arrestees tested positive) and Nottingham (just under one-third of arrestees tested positive). The highest rates for cocaine were also in Liverpool with 40 per cent of arrestees testing positive for the drug and Nottingham with about one-quarter of arrestees testing positive. The consumption of methadone was lower overall with about one-fifth of arrestees testing positive in Liverpool and six per cent in Nottingham.

The percentage of positive tests for cannabis was fairly constant across the four sites ranging from 43 per cent in Liverpool to 54 per cent in Sunderland. Detection of alcohol was also fairly constant across sites ranging from 17 per cent (Nottingham) to 26 per cent (South Norwood). The tendency for sites with high levels of use of opiates and cocaine to have low levels of alcohol use, found in the first-developmental stage of the research, is also evident in the current sites (with the exception of Liverpool which had the highest rate of opiate and cocaine use, but only the third lowest rate of alcohol use). The prevalence of positive tests for amphetamine use tended to be lower than the other drugs, although over one-fifth of all arrestees in Sunderland tested positive for this drug. The percentage of positive tests for benzodiazepines (such as temazepam and diazepam) was also slightly lower. However, almost one-fifth of arrestees in the Liverpool site tested positive for this type of drug.

Figure 4.1: *Percentage positive tests among arrestees, excluding alcohol*

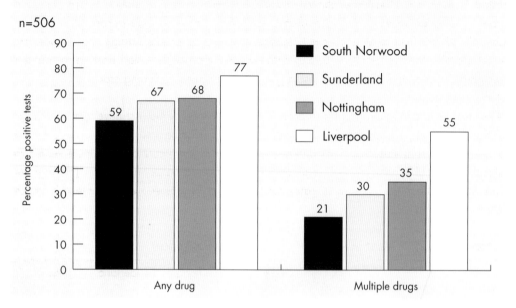

Figure 4.2: *Percentage positive tests among arrestees for selected drug types*

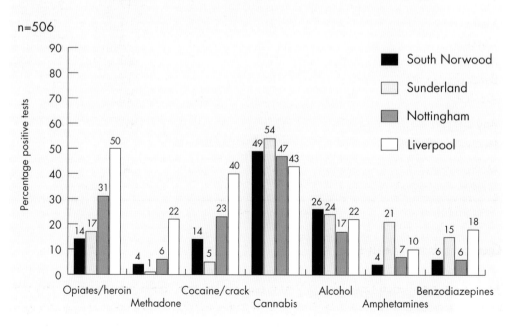

Table 4.1 presents the same results in tabular form showing the total number of arrestees tested in each site. The table allows comparison across sites in relation to specific drug types. It also provides a total prevalence rate for each drug type across all locations. Overall, 69 per cent of all arrestees tested positive for one or more drugs and 36 per cent tested positive for two or more. Twenty-nine percent of arrestees tested positive for opiates (including heroin) and 20 per cent tested positive for cocaine (including crack).

These rates are all higher than those presented in the report of the first developmental stage of the programme. It cannot be inferred from this that drug use has increased, as the package of sites in stage one was different to those in stage two. However, there were two sites that were also surveyed two years earlier at exactly the same time of year (Nottingham and Sunderland). The change in rates for these two sites is shown in Table 4.2 in the following section.

Table 4.1 :   Percentage positive tests among arrestees by area

	South Norwood n=73	Liverpool n=132	Nottingham n=132	Sunderland n=169	Total n=506
Cannabis	49	43	47	54	49
Opiates	14	50	31	17	29
Methadone	4	22	6	1	8
Cocaine	14	40	23	5	20
Amphetamines	4	10	7	21	12
Benzodiazepines	6	18	6	15	12
Alcohol	26	22	17	24	22
Any drug [excluding alcohol]	59	77	68	67	69
Multiple drugs [excluding alcohol]	21	55	35	30	36

Notes: [1] Includes only those arrestees who provided a specimen.

Changes in drug use over time

There is clear evidence from Table 4.2 of a general increase in the prevalence of drug use among arrestees, as measured by the results of urine testing. In both areas the percentages of arrestees testing positive for cannabis increased (the increase was statistically significant in Sunderland, but not in Nottingham). In Nottingham, the prevalence of positive tests for opiates and cocaine increased by a significant amount. In Sunderland the percentage of positive tests for opiates and cocaine also increased, but just failed to reach statistical significance (using a 95% confidence level). However, the increase in cocaine was statistically significant at a reduced (80%) level of certainty. Hence, there is an 80 per cent chance (but not a 95 per cent chance) that the increase in cocaine use in Sunderland was real (i.e. unrelated to sampling error).

The prevalence of amphetamine use changed in different ways across the two sites. The proportion of arrestees testing positive for amphetamines increased significantly in Sunderland and decreased in Nottingham (not statistically significant). Similarly, the percentage of arrestees testing positive for benzodiazepines increased in Sunderland, but decreased slightly in Nottingham (neither change was statistically significant).

It is perhaps more revealing to consider these changes in more detail across a range of drugs. The pattern of change in Nottingham is more clear-cut than that shown for Sunderland. There is clear evidence that consumption of the major Class A drugs (opiates including heroin, and cocaine including crack) substantially increased in the survey area. There is very little change (perhaps a slight increase) in the use of cannabis. However, there appears to be a possible reduction in the use of amphetamines, benzodiazepines and alcohol. The overall increase in any drug use and multiple drug use can almost entirely be explained by the increases shown in the Class A drugs. Hence, it might be hypothesised that the pattern of drug use in Nottingham has switched from the 'minor' to the 'major' drugs over the two year period of the surveys. This represents in some senses a 'hardening' of drug use in the area and may well reflect a more general change in patterns of drug use.

The pattern of change in Sunderland is different and more complex. In this case, there is strong evidence of an increase in cannabis use and in amphetamine and benzodiazepine use (almost the opposite to that shown in Nottingham). Conversely, there may also have been a small increase in the use of opiates and cocaine. However, these changes have been so slight that they fail to reach normal levels of statistical significance. The differences between the two areas might be explained by their different starting points. In 1997, Sunderland arrestees were characterised by high levels of alcohol use and relatively little involvement in other forms of drug use. By 1999, the prevalence of positive tests for alcohol had declined significantly and the prevalence of positive tests for the 'minor' drugs had increased significantly. However, there was less strong evidence of change among the 'major' drugs, which showed either no change or a small increase.

It is possible that the two areas are in fact moving in similar ways, but from different starting points. Arrestees in Nottingham were more likely to test positive for most drug types in 1997 than Sunderland arrestees. The escalation in drug use in Nottingham moved from 'minor' to 'major' drugs. Sunderland arrestees were more likely to test positive for alcohol in 1997 than were Nottingham arrestees. The escalation in drug use in Sunderland moved from alcohol to 'minor' drugs. Without further comparisons, these interpretations remain speculative. However, they both point to a worsening of drug misuse among currently active offenders in the two research locations.

Table 4.2 : *Trends in percentage positive tests among arrestees over time: 1997 and 1999*

(Percentages)

	Nottingham			Sunderland		
	1997	1999	Significance of difference	1997	1999	Significance of difference
	n=132	n=132		n=209	n=169	
Cannabis	42	47		36	54	*** (+)
Opiates	16	31	** (+)	13	17	
Methadone	6	6		1	1	
Cocaine	10	23	** (+)	1	5	
Amphetamines	13	7		9	21	** (+)
Benzodiazepines	7	6		11	15	
Alcohol	23	17		43	24	*** (-)
Any drug [excluding alcohol]	55	68		49	67	*** (+)
Multiple drugs [excluding alcohol]	24	35		17	30	*** (+)

Notes: [1] Includes only those arrestees who provided a specimen. *= p<.05; **= p<.01; ***=p<.001 Chi-squared test: corrected for 2X2 tables, where appropriate. (+) and (-) show the direction of change.

Drug use among different social groups

A great deal more information can be obtained from the results of the urinalysis by examining prevalence rates for different types of arrestee. Table 4.3 shows the breakdown in test results by sex, age and ethnic group, across the four sites.

Males are much more likely than females to test positive for cannabis and alcohol. However, females are significantly more likely than males to test positive for opiates and cocaine. In fact, just under a half (45%) of all females across all sites tested positive for opiates and almost one-third (30%) tested positive for cocaine. A similar pattern was found in the first developmental stage of the research covering five locations. While only 13 per cent of the arrestees were female, their high level of use of opiates and cocaine should be of some significance when considering drugs prevention policy.

Table 4.3 also shows that there is a strong correlation between testing positive for various drug types and age. Younger arrestees (aged under 25) were much more likely than older arrestees (aged 25 and over) to test positive for cannabis and for any drug (largely as a result of their high levels of cannabis use). However, older arrestees were much more likely than younger arrestees to test positive for the Class A drugs, including opiates, methadone and cocaine. Older arrestees were also more likely than younger ones to test positive for amphetamines. Almost identical findings (using slightly different age groupings) were presented in the report of the first developmental stage.

It should be noted that these findings (that use of opiates and cocaine is more prevalent among older arrestees) should not be taken to mean that the government strategy to focus on younger people (aged under 25) is misplaced. Almost one-third of all arrestees aged 20 to 24 tested positive for opiates and just over one-fifth (22%) of this group tested positive for cocaine. There is also evidence of increased use of these two drug types with age. Attempts to reduce the prevalence of use of this type of drug among the younger age group might eventually help reduce the prevalence of use among the older age group.

In terms of ethnicity, contrasts were more muted. The only significant differences between the groups were that white arrestees were more likely than non-white arrestees to test positive for opiates and amphetamines. The prevalence of cannabis and cocaine use was identical. In relation to the remaining drug types, there is some tendency for whites to have higher prevalence rates than non-whites (although none of the remaining relationships was statistically significant). Hence, the results tend to show that white arrestees are either more involved or equally involved in drug use as non-whites.

This finding is slightly different to those of the first developmental stage report which showed that non-whites were more likely than whites to test positive for cannabis and cocaine. It is possible, therefore, that the relationship between ethnic group and drug use varies by location. It should be possible to explain this relationship more fully when the results of all 16 sites of the NEW-ADAM programme are available.

Table 4.3: Percentage positive tests among arrestees by sex, age and ethnic group

| | Sex | | | Age | | | | Ethnic group | |
| | Males | Females | 17–19 | 20–24 | 25–29 | 30–59 | White | Non-white |
n=506	n=439	n=67	n=116	n=125	n=101	n=164	n=457	n=49
Cannabis	51	33 **	73	50	43	34 ***	49	49
Opiates	26	45 **	10	32	39	33 ***	31	12 *
Methadone	8	10	1	6	11	13 ***	9	2
Cocaine	19	30 *	10	22	29	20 **	20	20
Amphetamines	11	19	7	9	13	17 *	13	0 *
Benzodiazepines	12	12	5	14	15	14	13	4
Alcohol	24	10 *	22	20	18	26	22	20
Any drug [excluding alcohol]	68	75	78	71	71	59 **	69	61
Multiple drugs [excluding alcohol]	35	43	23	38	49	37 **	38	18 *

Notes: [1] Includes only those arrestees who provided a specimen. * p<.05; ** p<.01; ***p<.001 Chi-squared test: corrected for 2X2 tables, where appropriate.

Drug use and offending

The relationship between testing positive for drugs and selected offence types is shown in Table 4.4. Looking first at opiates, it shows that around two-thirds of all arrestees held for shoplifting and burglary of a shop or office or other non-dwelling tested positive for this group of drugs. Exactly one-fifth of all arrestees held for burglary in a dwelling tested positive for opiates and about one-quarter held for robbery tested positive. These rates for opiates are all higher than those reported in the first developmental stage report. The reason for the difference is in part the different package of research sites (including Liverpool with very high prevalence rates of drug use) and in part a real change over time as identified in the trend comparison for Nottingham and to a lesser extent Sunderland. In Nottingham, the proportion of arrestees held for shoplifting who tested positive for opiates increased from 38 per cent in 1997 to 63 per cent in 1999.

Looking at the prevalence of positive tests for cocaine shows that the highest rates were for the same two offences: 41 per cent of those held for shoplifting tested positive and 50 per cent of those held for burglary non-dwelling. One-quarter of arrestees held for robbery tested positive for cocaine and 20 per cent of those held for fraud or deception. Again, these rates are much higher than those in the first report and are also a product of a combination of both the different package of locations and real changes over time.

Table 4.4: Percentage positive tests among arrestees held for common offence types

	Cannabis	Opiates	Methadone	Cocaine	Amphetamines	Benzodiazepines	Alcohol	Any drug (excl. alcohol)	Multiple drugs (excl. alcohol)	Total arrestees held for specific offence
Assault	34	24	7	12	10	10	32	61	27	41
Robbery	75	25	25	25	0	0	75	100	25	4
Burglary dwelling	56	20	4	8	16	24	8	76	32	25
Burglary non-dwelling	33	67	8	50	17	42	17	83	67	12
Theft from vehicle	50	0	0	0	0	0	0	50	0	2
Theft of/taking vehicle	68	16	8	19	11	19	30	78	38	37
Theft shoplifting	60	64	33	41	17	26	7	86	74	42
Theft other	52	36	3	13	16	13	13	81	36	31
Handling	50	25	0	0	25	50	25	50	50	4
Fraud/deception	20	20	0	20	20	0	0	40	20	5
Criminal damage	46	25	8	8	21	4	29	58	33	24
Drugs supply	75	38	0	25	0	13	13	88	25	8
Drugs possession	74	28	2	28	21	5	26	86	47	43
Breach of the peace	17	11	0	0	11	6	61	33	11	18

Notes: Includes only those arrestees who provided a specimen and were held for the offences shown. Arrestees held for more than one offence have been coded in terms of the most serious offence using the scale published by Phillips and Brown (1998). The full table is shown in Appendix B, Table B4.1.

In addition to the urine specimen collection and analysis, arrestees were asked during the interview about their drug use. There are a number of advantages to asking arrestees to report on their drug misuse. It is possible to examine use over longer periods of time than can be measured using urinalysis. It enables more information to be collected about a wider range of drug types. It is also possible to ask arrestees related questions concerning age of first use (one of the performance indicators in the first strand of the government's drugs strategy) and dependency (one of the performance indicators in the third strand of the government's drugs strategy). In this chapter, only the results relating to the first objective will be discussed. The results relating to dependency and treatment will be presented in later chapters.

The percentage of arrestees reporting using each of 21 drug types in the last 12 months is shown in Table 5.1. The table also compares the prevalence rates for arrestees aged 17 to 59 with the rates of the general population aged 16 to 59 found in the last British Crime Survey (bearing in mind that the general population and the arrestee population are likely to be quite different in other ways). The table shows that tobacco and alcohol are the most commonly consumed drugs, used by over 80 per cent of arrestees in the last 12 months. The most commonly consumed illegal drug was cannabis, used by 67 per cent of arrestees (seven times the prevalence rate of the general population). This was followed by amphetamines, which were used by 32 per cent of arrestees in the last year, compared with three per cent of the general population (a ratio of 11:1). Heroin use was reported by 28 per cent of arrestees, compared with less than 0.5 per cent of the general population, and cocaine use was reported by 26 per cent of arrestees compared with one per cent of the general population.

Table 5.1:   Self-reported drug use in the last 12 months among arrestees aged 17 to 59

	NEW-ADAM: 1998-99	BCS: 1998: 16–59	
	All 17–59	All 16–59	Ratio of general population to all arrestees aged 17 to 59
n=	738 [1]		
Amphetamines	32	3	1:11
Cannabis	67	9	1:7
Cocaine	26	1	1:26
Crack	25	*	
Ecstasy	17	1	1:17
Heroin	28	*	
LSD	7	1	1:7
Magic mushrooms	6	1	1:6
Methadone	15	*	
Steroids	1	*	
Temazepam	15	-	
Diazepam	18	-	
Other tranquillisers	8	-	
Barbiturates	2	-	
Diconal	2	-	
DF118s	14	-	
Temgesic	3	-	
Amyl nitrite	7	1	1:7
Solvents	2	*	
Tobacco	86	-	
Alcohol	83	-	
Any drug exc. alcohol and tobacco	76	-	
Multiple drugs exc. alcohol and tobacco	57	-	

Note: [1] Two arrestees fell outside of the age range 17 to 59. '*'=Less than 0.5%; '-' no comparison.

Table 5.2: Self-reported drug use over various periods of time by age

n=738 [1]

Period	17–24 age group % ever	17–24 % last 12 months	17–24 % last 30 days	17–24 % last 3 days	25–59 age group % ever	25–59 % last 12 months	25–59 % last 30 days	25–59 % last 3 days	Significance of difference Ever	Sig. last 12 months	Sig. last 30 days	Sig. last 3 days
Amphetamines	62	36	17	6	58	28	17	10		*		*+
Cannabis	85	77	71	59	75	59	52	37	**-	***-	***-	***-
Cocaine	34	25	14	5	40	26	15	9				*+
Crack	27	23	17	9	33	27	22	15				*+
Ecstasy	46	23	14	4	41	12	7	1	**+	***-		**-
Heroin	28	22	18	15	40	34	30	26	**+	***+	***+	***+
LSD	50	10	3	1	45	5	1	1		*-		
Magic Mushrooms	29	8	2	2	35	4	1	-		*-		
Methadone	13	7	5	1	29	22	15	11	***+	***+	***+	***+
Steroids	5	2	-	-	5	-	-	-				
Temazepam	26	14	8	4	34	15	9	4	*+			
Diazepam	23	15	8	5	31	20	10	6	*+			
Other tranquillisers	8	6	3	1	21	11	6	2	***+	*+	*+	
Barbiturates	5	2	1	1	8	2	1	-				
Diconal	2	2	1	-	6	1	1	-	*+			
DF118s	16	10	5	2	26	17	9	5	**+	*+		*+
Temgesic	10	4	-	-	13	3	1	-				
Amyl nitrite	39	10	6	1	31	3	2	1	*-	***-	**-	
Solvents	25	2	1	-	20	1	1	-				
Tobacco	90	86	86	83	90	86	85	84				
Alcohol	91	89	85	61	86	78	70	54	*-	***-	***-	***-
Any drug exc. alcohol and tobacco	89	82	78	67	82	71	65	57	*-	***-	***-	**-
Multiple drugs exc. alcohol and tobacco	77	59	43	26	71	55	45	34				*+

Note: [1] Two arrestees fell outside of the age range 17 to 59. '-' = less than 0.5%. The significance of the difference among younger and older arrestees is indicated by a symbol and a sign shown in the relevant column relating to the older group. * p<.05; ** p<.01; ***p<.001 Chi-squared test: corrected for 2X2 tables. (+) and (-) = direction of difference.

The second table in this chapter (Table 5.2) has been split into two age groups, 17 to 24 and 25 to 59 to match the main age groups reported in the last British Crime Survey report on drug misuse in the general population (Ramsay and Partridge, 1999) and to identify the same group of young people (aged under 25) referred to in the government's drugs strategy.

Younger (17 to 24) arrestees were more likely than older (25 to 59) arrestees to say that they had used amphetamines in their lifetime (62% compared with 58%) and in the last 12 months (36% compared with 28%). However, older arrestees were more likely than younger arrestees to say that they had used amphetamines recently (10% compared with 6%). This variation across different time periods could be explained by a recent increase in use of amphetamines among older arrestees. The recent increase in amphetamine use in Sunderland, observed in the urinalysis findings, lends support to this view.

Younger arrestees were significantly more likely than older arrestees to have consumed cannabis. Over 80 per cent of younger arrestees (85%) and three-quarters of older arrestees (75%) said that they had used cannabis at least once in their lifetime. Fifty-nine per cent of the younger group and 37 per cent of the older group had done so in the last three days. The higher percentage of younger than older arrestees using the drug in their lifetime is interesting, as older arrestees have had longer lifetimes than younger arrestees to try the drug. This finding supports the conclusion of the latest British Crime Survey, which suggests that young people in general are currently more likely than young people of the past (including those growing up in the 1960s and the 'hippie' era of drug experimentation) to have used cannabis.

About one-third (34%) of the younger group of arrestees and 40 per cent of the older group said that they had consumed cocaine at some time in their lives. Overall, older arrestees were more likely than younger ones to report using cocaine (the difference was significant in relation to use in the last three days). Slightly fewer of each group said that they had used crack (27% and 33%) in their lifetime. Again, older arrestees were more likely to report using the drug than younger arrestees.

There is little evidence that crack/cocaine has begun to rival heroin as the 'major' drug of preference. It is true that the prevalence patterns of the three drugs are fairly similar over the whole lifetime, in the last 12 months and in the last 30 days. However, the reported rates of heroin use in the last three days are much higher than the rates of cocaine or crack use in the last three days. This difference is almost certainly a result of higher rates of use of heroin over crack and cocaine (discussed in more detail later in this chapter). In relation to each time period comparison, the older group was more likely than the younger group to report using the drug. Similar results are obtained for use of methadone (a heroin substitute) which was also far more common among older than younger arrestees.

This pattern of greater involvement of older arrestees in the 'harder' drugs (e.g. heroin, crack and cocaine and their substitutes) and greater involvement of younger arrestees in the 'softer' drugs (e.g. cannabis) is repeated in other parts of the table. It was also shown in the results of the urinalysis which produced similar findings. For example, older arrestees were more likely than younger arrestees to report using diconal and DF118s (heroin substitutes), whereas younger arrestees were more likely to report using ecstasy and LSD (not all comparisons were statistically significant).

The fact that younger arrestees are less involved in using the more dangerous drugs does not mean that drug use among this group is unproblematic. First, drug use prevalence among young arrestees is still very high and much higher than has been found among the same age group in the general population (Ramsay and Partridge, 1999). Second, the use of even the less damaging illicit drugs, coupled with their high levels of consumption of alcohol and tobacco, exposes them to some of the problems of drug misuse.

Changes in self-reported drug use over time

Table 5.3 examines changes in reported drug use over time and focuses on the results of the Nottingham and Sunderland surveys. As the surveys were conducted in the same month exactly two years apart and using the same questionnaire and the same method of sampling, they provide a further opportunity to monitor with some confidence changes in drug use in these locations over time.

Table 5.3 : **Trends in self-reported drug use in the last 12 months among arrestees over time: 1997 and 1999**

	Nottingham			Sunderland		
	1997	1999	Significance of difference	1997	1999	Significance of difference
	n=209	n=204		n=271	n=182	
Amphetamines	49	35	** (-)	44	47	
Cannabis	70	71		59	68	[1] (+)
Cocaine	17	12		14	17	
Crack	20	31	** (+)	7	11	
Ecstasy	28	13	*** (-)	26	22	
Heroin	24	37	** (+)	10	17	[1] (+)
LSD	23	5	*** (-)	18	11	[1] (-)
Magic mushrooms	9	8		11	7	
Methadone	16	17		8	6	
Temazepam	22	10	** (-)	28	22	
Diazepam	14	14		23	24	
Other tranquillisers	15	11		12	7	[1] (-)
Barbiturates	3	2		4	3	
Diconal	4	1		1	3	
DF118s	11	13		9	13	
Temgesic	4	2		15	9	[1] (-)
Amyl nitrite	22	4	*** (-)	16	14	
Solvents	6	3		4	2	
Tobacco	89	89		82	83	
Alcohol	89	81	* (-)	95	89	* (-)
Any drug exc. alcohol and tobacco	81	78		67	78	* (+)
Multiple drugs exc. alcohol and tobacco	65	57		54	59	

Notes: *= p<.05; **= p<.01; ***=p<.001 Chi-squared test: corrected for 2X2 tables, where appropriate. (+) and (-) show the direction of change. Arrestees were not asked about steroids in 1997 in either survey. [1] significant at a reduced confidence level of p<.1.

The table provides additional information to the results of the urinalysis discussed earlier. The urinalysis showed that opiate use and cocaine use had increased in Nottingham. The prevalence of self-reported heroin use had also increased significantly (confirming the increase in opiate use revealed by urinalysis was in fact an increase in heroin use) and that the prevalence of crack use had likewise increased significantly (indicating that the increase in cocaine use revealed by urinalysis was in fact the result of an increase in the use of crack cocaine rather than powder cocaine).

The results of the urinalysis for Sunderland showed an increase in the percentage of arrestees testing positive for opiates and cocaine. However, neither change was statistically significant and it was unknown whether the recorded difference was meaningful. The results of the self-report analysis shown above repeat this finding. The table shows that there were percentage increases in the prevalence of crack, cocaine and heroin use. However, none of the changes was statistically significant at the normal confidence level. However, the increase in heroin use was significant at a reduced confidence level (with a 90% rather than the normal 95% chance that the difference was unrelated to sampling error). In conclusion, there is no firm evidence of an increase in prevalence of these 'major' drugs in Sunderland, although there are some faint signs that use may be increasing.

High-rate users

Table 5.4 examines rates of use of the different drug types in the four survey areas. The table compares the proportion of high-rate users in relation to each drug. The term 'high-rate' is defined as meaning that the drug was used 15 days or more in the last 30 days (i.e. at least every other day on average).

**Table 5.4:   Percentage of high rate users (used 15 days or more in the last 30 days)
among all users**

	South Norwood	Liverpool	Nottingham	Sunderland	All 17 to 59	Total number of users
Amphetamines	21	17	31	26	25	126
Cannabis	57	60	61	57	59	448
Cocaine	29	38	6	25	30	107
Crack	52	57	35	30	47	145
Ecstasy	0	10	8	6	7	73
Heroin	69	79	71	60	73	177
LSD	0	33	0	0	15	13
Magic mushrooms	0	0	33	0	9	11
Methadone	56	63	37	25	53	75
Steroids	0	50	0	0	25	4
Temazepam	40	14	42	22	25	65
Diazepam	0	29	8	42	28	65
Other tranquillisers	0	31	25	33	27	33
Barbiturates	0	0	100	0	17	6
Diconal	0	0	0	0	0	6
DF118s	0	17	30	25	21	53
Temgesic	0	0	0	17	13	8
Amyl nitrite	0	14	0	0	4	28
Solvents	0	0	25	0	17	6
Tobacco	93	98	92	93	94	630
Alcohol	36	34	34	37	35	568

Note: Rates refer only to users of the specific drug type in the last 30 days aged 17-59.

The table shows that the percentage of high-rate users was greatest (exceeding 50% of users) in relation to cannabis, heroin, methadone and tobacco. Nearly three-quarters (73%) of all heroin users and half (53%) of all methadone users said that they used the drug on average at least every other day. Fifty-nine per cent of cannabis users were high-rate users and over 90 per cent of tobacco users fell in this category. The percentage of high-rate users was in the middle of the range (between 25% and 50% of users) in relation to amphetamines, crack, cocaine, steroids, diazepam, temazepam, other tranquillisers, and alcohol. Just under half (47%) of crack users and just under one-third (30%) of cocaine users were classified as high-rate users. The percentage of high-rate users was lowest (less than 25% of users) in relation to ecstasy, LSD, magic mushrooms, barbiturates, diconal, DF118s, temgesic, amyl nitrite and solvents. Comparing the findings across locations for 'major' drug use shows that Liverpool was ranked at the top in terms of having the highest rates of use of crack, cocaine and heroin (in addition to ranking highest in terms of prevalence of use of these drugs, as discussed earlier).

The rate of use of each of the drug types is important in evaluating the connection between various kinds of problem behaviour, including the connection between drugs and crime. Heroin traditionally has been the drug most commonly associated with problem behaviour in the British context, not only because of its prevalence of use, but also because of the high rates of use among those who became dependent upon it. So far, a lower proportion of users of cocaine and crack fall into this high-rate category.

Age of onset

The final table in this chapter examines the changes in the age of onset of drug misuses over time in relation to the Nottingham and Sunderland surveys. This table has been included because it is one of the government's aims to delay the age of onset of Class A drugs by six months over the next two years. Table 5.5 lists the reported age of onset of all of the main drug types covered in the survey. The table shows that in 1997 the mean age of onset of crack, cocaine and heroin use in both Nottingham and Sunderland was about 20 to 21 years of age. In Nottingham, the mean age of onset reduced slightly in relation to cocaine, but increased by a very small amount (representing delays in onset of between two or three months) in relation to crack and heroin. In Sunderland, the mean age of onset of heroin use reduced slightly, but increased by a slightly larger amount in relation to cocaine and crack (representing a delay in onset in excess of six months).

It is probably too early to comment on this change. The current number of comparison sites is too small to observe any kind of trend and the number of cases in the combined sample is too few to have the power to detect a statistically significant change in the order of six months. However, as the NEW-ADAM programme develops, a greater number of comparisons will be possible and a greater combined dataset will be generated which will be better able to measure small changes of this kind.

Table 5.5: *Trends in age of onset of self-reported drug use in the last 12 months among arrestees over time: 1997 and 1999*

	Nottingham			Sunderland		
	1997	1999	Significance of difference	1997	1999	Significance of difference
	n=209	n=204		n=271	n=182	
Amphetamines	18.0	17.1	ns	17.2	19.0	** (+)
Cannabis	15.9	15.7	ns	15.9	16.6	ns
Cocaine	20.8	20.5	ns	20.5	21.1	ns
Crack	21.3	21.6	ns	21.7	23.8	ns
Ecstasy	20.6	19.6	ns	18.9	19.3	ns
Heroin	20.5	20.7	ns	21.9	21.7	ns
LSD	17.4	17.0	ns	16.4	17.3	ns
Magic mushrooms	18.2	17.7	ns	17.4	18.1	ns
Methadone	23.3	22.9	ns	22.7	25.1	ns
Temazepam	21.4	20.7	ns	18.7	19.7	ns
Diazepam	22.0	22.0	ns	19.4	20.4	ns
Other tranquillisers	22.0	21.6	ns	20.7	23.5	ns
Barbiturates	19.9	19.5	ns	17.7	17.5	ns
Diconal	23.3	27.8	ns	21.4	18.9	ns
DF118s	22.2	22.3	ns	19.6	21.1	ns
Temgesic	23.8	22.0	ns	19.5	21.0	ns
Amyl nitrite	18.7	17.6	ns	17.4	17.1	ns
Solvents	14.9	14.5	ns	13.6	14.2	ns
Tobacco	13.8	14.3	ns	13.7	14.1	ns
Alcohol	14.0	14.5	ns	14.5	15.1	* (+)

Notes: [1] Includes only those arrestees who reported using the drug at least once in their lives. *= p<.05; **= p<.01; ***=p<.001; ns=not significant. Chi-squared test: corrected for 2X2 tables, where appropriate. (+) and (-) show the direction of change. Arrestees were not asked about steroids in 1997 in either survey.

Expenditure on drugs

The amount spent on drugs provides another indicator of the prevalence of drug misuse among arrestees. Expenditure on drugs can also indicate the regularity of use of drugs and the frequency of involvement in the process of seeking and purchasing drugs. Levels of expenditure on drugs can also tell us something about the link between drug use and crime. Arrestees who use large quantities of drugs must find some way of generating the funds to pay for them. There is an obvious danger that at least some of these funds will be generated from crime.

Arrestees who reported that they had used at least one drug (excluding alcohol and tobacco) in the last 12 months were asked how much they had spent on drugs in the last seven days. Table 6.1 presents the average levels of expenditure on drugs among arrestees over this period. Combining the four survey areas shows that the average weekly expenditure on drugs, among all arrestees who had consumed at least one illegal drug in the last 12 months, was £129. This figure is deflated slightly by the inclusion of arrestees who spent no money on drugs in the last week. The higher-rate users will obviously spend much more than this. The average amount spent varied slightly across areas. The highest expenditure was in Liverpool (an average of £192 per week) and the lowest was in Sunderland (an average of £72 per week).

Looking at variations among different groups of arrestees shows that females tended to report higher levels of expenditure on drugs than males in three of the four locations, with an average expenditure of £171 per week. This finding is almost certainly linked to the higher rate of use among females of opiates and cocaine (the most expensive and addictive drugs).

Younger arrestees (aged under 25) tended to report lower levels of expenditure than older arrestees (aged 25 to 59). Overall, the average expenditure on drugs among younger arrestees was £106 compared with £153 among older arrestees (the difference was statistically significant). The relationship between age and expenditure was consistent across three of the four sites (although was statistically significant only in Liverpool). However, in the Sunderland site, younger arrestees spent a larger amount on drugs than older arrestees. It would appear that the difference in expenditure patterns among younger and older arrestees is almost certainly affected by the overall pattern of drug use in the area. The prevalence rate of the 'major' drugs (typically associated with use among older arrestees) was much lower in

Sunderland than in the other areas. Conversely, the prevalence of use of the 'minor' drugs (typically associated with use among younger arrestees) was much higher in Sunderland.

In two of the four areas, the small number of non-white arrestees in the sample precluded any kind of comparison in terms of drug expenditure. In one of the remaining two areas (South Norwood), white arrestees reported higher levels of expenditure than non-white arrestees and in the other (Nottingham) the reverse was the case (in neither area was the difference statistically significant).

Table 6.1: **Mean expenditure on drugs over the last seven days by sex, age and ethnic group**

		South Norwood n=94 £	Liverpool n=167 £	Nottingham n=160 £	Sunderland n=142 £	All 17-59 n=563 £	Total n of users n=563
Sex	Male	103	179	119	76	123ns	486
	Female	220	275	156	48	171	77
Age	17–24	56	129 *	119	96	106 *	285
	25–59	157	245	134	43	153	278
Ethnic group	White	148	188	119	72	132ns	498
	Non-white	54	-	156	-	110	65
All users		112	192	125	72	129	563

Notes:Includes only arrestees aged 17–59. Mean expenditure on drugs is based on arrestees who said that they had consumed at least one drug type in the last 12 months excluding alcohol or tobacco. Mean expenditure includes cases of zero expenditure. Includes all amounts as reported with no high-end cut-off. * p<.05; ** p<.01; ***p<.001; ns=not significant. T-Test. '-' = less than 5 cases.

Table 6.2 examines differences in expenditure patterns in relation to different types of drug use. The drug-using sub-groups shown are based on the logical combinations of heroin and crack/cocaine use. The divisions is not intended to represent known patterns of drug use or to suggest a meaningful drug-use typology. Instead, the choice of drugs reflects current academic and policy concerns relating to the possible connection between heroin and crack/cocaine use and crime.

Arrestees who used both heroin and crack/cocaine in the last 12 months reported the highest levels of expenditure on drugs of all groups. Overall, the mean expenditure in the last seven days among users of both heroin and crack/cocaine was £308, which represents ten times the expenditure of arrestees who did not use these drugs. It is also more than three times the amount spent among users of just heroin or crack/cocaine. Users of heroin alone and users of crack/cocaine alone reported higher levels of expenditure than users of other drugs and lower levels than users of both drugs. However, there was little difference in terms of whether the arrestee specialised in heroin or crack/cocaine use.

The average amount spent on drugs among users of heroin and crack/cocaine varied slightly across the areas. The highest weekly expenditure rates were in South Norwood and Liverpool (the two metropolitan sites) (over £400 a week and £300 a week respectively). The difference in expenditure rates across areas can be the result of a number of factors, including the prevalence of use, rate of use and cost of drugs. Estimates from the National Criminal Intelligence Service (NCIS) for 1999 suggest that heroin and crack/cocaine prices were slightly lower in Liverpool than the other sites and slightly higher in London (Liverpool prices were £40–£60 per gram of heroin and £40–£50 per gram of cocaine and London prices were £60–£80 for heroin and £60–£120 for cocaine). Hence, it is possible that the higher rates of expenditure among users of heroin and crack/cocaine in South Norwood was in part explained by higher price and the higher rates in Liverpool was in part explained by the higher prevalence and frequency of use. These factors obviously play some part in determining the nature of the drugs-crime connection.

Table 6.2: **Mean expenditure on drugs over the last seven days by type of drugs used**

	South Norwood n=94 £	Liverpool n=167 £	Nottingham n=160 £	Sunderland n=142 £	All 17-59 n=563 £	Total n of users n=563
Neither heroin nor crack/cocaine use	46	33	26	25	31	247
Heroin use – no crack/cocaine use	20	118	71	100	89	41
Crack/cocaine use – no heroin use	65	149	83	57	93	107
Heroin and crack/ cocaine use	415	327	265	284	308	168
All users	112***	192 ***	125***	72***	129 ***	563

Notes:Includes only arrestees aged 17–59. Mean expenditure on drugs is based on arrestees who said that they had consumed at least one drug type in the last 12 months excluding alcohol or tobacco. Mean expenditure includes cases of zero expenditure. Includes all amounts as reported with no high-end cut-off. * p<.05; ** p<.01; ***p<.001; ns=not significant. T-Test.

The next table (Table 6.3) combines prevalence rate and price in a single measure by examining the total amount spent on drugs among each group as a whole. The table shows that the total expenditure of users of heroin and crack/cocaine constituted over 70 per cent of the total expenditure on drugs of all arrestees, whereas heroin and crack/cocaine users constituted 30 per cent of the total number of arrestees.

Table 6.3:   Total expenditure on drugs over the last seven days by type of drugs used

£s

	Total spent by group	Percentage of total spent	Percentage of total users	Total number users
Neither heroin nor crack/cocaine use	7,526	10	44	247
Heroin use – no crack/cocaine use	3,647	5	7	41
Crack/cocaine use – no heroin use	10,000	14	19	107
Heroin and crack/cocaine use	51,730	71	30	168
All users	72,903	100	100	563

Notes:Includes only arrestees aged 17–59. Mean expenditure on drugs is based on arrestees who said that they had consumed at least one drug type in the last 12 months excluding alcohol or tobacco. Mean expenditure includes cases of zero expenditure. Includes all amounts as reported with no high-end cut-off.

Table 6.4 looks at changes in expenditure on drugs over time by comparing the results of the repeat surveys in Nottingham and Sunderland. The table shows that mean expenditure on drugs among users of both heroin and crack/cocaine increased slightly in Nottingham over the period 1997 to 1999 and decreased slightly in Sunderland. In neither area was the change statistically significant. Similarly, there were both small increases and small decreases in expenditure among users of heroin or crack/cocaine alone across the survey sites, none of which reached statistical significance.

It might have been expected that the increase in prevalence in both heroin use and crack/cocaine in Nottingham (but not in Sunderland) would have resulted in an increase in mean (average) expenditure on drugs. However, this need not necessarily be the case. Mean expenditure is a function of total expenditure (or price per unit multiplied by number of units purchased) and number of users. If price per unit and number of units purchased per user remained constant, then an increase in the number of users would not affect mean expenditure on drugs.

Table 6.4: **Trends in mean expenditure on drugs in the last seven days among arrestees over time: 1997 and 1999**

£s

	Nottingham			Sunderland		
	1997	1999	Significance of difference	1997	1999	Significance of difference
	n=170	n=160		n=181	n=142	
	£	£		£	£	
Neither heroin nor crack/cocaine use	24	26	ns	22	25	ns
Heroin use – no crack/cocaine use	117	71	ns	112	100	ns
Crack/cocaine use – no heroin use	110	83	ns	45	57	ns
Heroin and crack/ cocaine use	241	265	ns	309	216	ns
All users	89	125	ns	61	63	ns

Notes:This table was compiled from the original force reports and the means for 1999 are slightly different to those presented earlier in this chapter. This is due to the inclusion of all arrestees (rather than just those aged 17–59) and the use of a high-end cut-off (which was not used in the tables shown earlier in this chapter). Mean values include cases with zero illegal income. * $p<.05$; ** $p<.01$; ***$p<.001$; ns=not significant. Chi-squared test: corrected for 2X2 tables, where appropriate. (+) and (-) show the direction of change.

Conclusion on drug misuse among arrestees

This section has covered issues relating to the rate and prevalence of drug misuse among arrestees and has paid particular attention to younger arrestees who are the focus of the first key objective of the current drugs strategy. While arrestees comprise a small proportion of all young people in the general population, they represent a particularly problematic group who, in some cases, engage in both drug use and crime.

The three chapters making up this part of the report have shown high levels of drug use among arrestees. Over two-thirds tested positive for one or more drugs (excluding alcohol and tobacco), over a quarter tested positive for opiates (including heroin), and about one-fifth tested positive for cocaine (including crack). Younger arrestees (aged under 25) were more likely than older arrestees to test positive for cannabis, while older arrestees were more likely than younger arrestees to test positive for opiates and cocaine. There was also some evidence from the Nottingham and Sunderland surveys of an increase in the use of opiates (particularly heroin use) and cocaine (particularly crack use) among arrestees over time.

The majority of arrestees who used heroin did so at a high rate (at least every other day) and just under one-half of arrestees who used cocaine or crack did so at least every other day. Arrestees who used both heroin and cocaine spent on average over £300 per week on drugs. In some areas, this group of arrestees spent in excess of £400 a week on drugs.

It is not an overstatement to say that drug misuse among arrestees is prolific. In one area (Liverpool), it was shown that half of the relevant arrestees tested positive for opiates and one-third tested positive for cocaine. An additional analysis of these results (not presented here) indicates that it is unlikely that the high rate of positive tests for opiates in Liverpool was a result of use of legitimate prescribed heroin. None of the arrestees in this location said that they had recently been given prescriptions for heroin. Further, 82 per cent of those who tested positive said that they had used illegal heroin in the last 3 days. These findings suggest that the most likely cause of the positive tests for opiates in this site was the use of illegal heroin.

These results support the government's decision to focus attention on the relationship between drug use and crime. Future NEW-ADAM surveys will provide authoritative monitoring of the prevalence of drug use among arrestees and will report on the impact of drugs policy in affecting prevalence rates over time.

Part Two: Drugs and crime

Key Performance Target Two

The second key performance target of the current drugs strategy is to reduce levels of repeat offending among drug-misusing offenders by 50 per cent by 2008 and 25 per cent by 2005.

The drugs–crime connection

The government's second key objective is based on the assumption that there is a connection between drug use and crime. It is also suggested in the above performance target that there is a hard core of drug misusers who offend at a particularly high rate. The NEW-ADAM programme (along with other especially collected drug use indicators) offers an opportunity to investigate the link between drug use and crime and an opportunity to monitor the connection between the two, both across areas and over time. However, before presenting the early results of the programme, it is worth considering what is already known from research about the drugs–crime connection.

The nature of the connection

There are at least five main explanations of the nature of the link between drugs and crime (see Collins et al., 1985; Otero-Lopez et al., 1994; or Bennett, 1991 for an overview). The first is the theory that drug use causes crime. Drug use might cause crime as a result of the psychopharmacological effects of the drug (whereby consumption of the drug leads directly or indirectly to the commission of crime) or as a result of what is referred to as 'economic necessity' (the consumption of illegal drugs is expensive and drug users typically have limited legal financial resources to fund them). The second is the theory that crime causes drug use. This is based on the idea that funds from crime can be spent on various pleasurable pursuits, including drug use. The third explanation is that drug use and crime are 'reciprocal'. On some occasions drug use causes crime and on some occasions crime causes drug use. The fourth explanation is that drug use and crime are both explained by a common cause. Some element of a situation, environment or deviant sub-culture might encourage both drug use and crime. The fifth explanation is known as the 'spuriousness model' which argues that drugs and crime are not causally connected at all, but simply co-exist within a complex setting of events which include both.

Evidence of a connection

There is a considerable body of research which has attempted to establish whether there is a statistical connection between drug use and crime. The association has been investigated in particular by looking at samples of criminals in order to determine their level of drug use and at samples of drug users in order to determine their level of criminality. The following comprises just a few highlights of this body of literature.

Studies which have attempted to determine drug use among samples of criminals have tended to focus on prisoners or arrestees. A study by Maden et al. (1992) of 1,751 male prisoners, found that about 43 per cent had misused drugs in the six-month period before entering prison. About one-third of these (34%) said that they had used cannabis and about five per cent said that they had used cocaine. Another study of the early period of mandatory drug testing conducted in five prisons in 1996 showed that the majority of prisoners (91%) admitted consuming at least one of a package of drugs at least once in their lifetimes. Eighty-eight per cent said that they had used cannabis, 45 per cent heroin and 50 per cent cocaine (Edgar and O'Donnell, 1998).

Studies of arrestees have mainly been conducted in the United States as part of the Drug Use Forecasting (DUF) and Arrestee Drug Abuse Monitoring (ADAM) programmes. The results published in the 1998 Annual Report of the ADAM programme, covering findings from 35 survey sites, show that about two-thirds of adult arrestees test positive for one or more drugs (National Institute of Justice, 1999). In 1998, the median rate of positive tests for cocaine was 37 per cent for adult male arrestees and 40 per cent for adult female arrestees. The median rates for positive tests for opiates were lower with the majority of sites reporting rates of ten per cent or lower.

The results of this body of research consistently show high levels of drug use among criminals. However, the findings need to be compared with another source in order to determine whether the rates are higher than expected among criminals. One option is to compare these rates with those of the general population (a summary of the results of general population surveys is shown in the introduction to the previous section). However, the general and criminal populations are different in many ways and the results of the comparison need to be treated with caution.

Studies which have attempted to determine levels of criminal behaviour among drug uses have typically focused on drug users in the community or drug users currently in treatment. A study by Inciardi et al. (1994) conducted in Miami, Florida of 699 cocaine users in the community found that the users reported 1.76 million offences in the last 90 days. The vast majority of these offences were related to drug dealing and other drug crimes. However, they also reported a very high number of other offences. Just under ten per cent of the sample admitted committing 3,223 robberies in the last 90 days (an average of one robbery per person every other day). The most common crimes admitted were selling stolen goods (15,746 offences), prostitution (15,802 offences) and con games (12,425 offences). A study by Hammersley et al. (1989) of 210 teenage drug users and non-drug users in Glasgow found that criminality among the group increased with increasing involvement in drug misuse. The most common crime committed among opioid users and among injectors was thefts. Opioid users committed thefts on average 37 days per year and injectors 108 days per year.

A treatment study by Jarvis and Parker (1989) of crime among young heroin users in London drew their sample from among users currently attending two Drug Dependency Units in London and from among known users currently serving a sentence of imprisonment in a London prison. The study found that the annual rate of conviction was higher among respondents during their 'post-heroin' period than in their 'pre-heroin' period. The most common offence committed among the heroin users in the last six months was shoplifting (committed by 41% of the sample) and cheque book fraud (24%). The research also found that there were relatively few weeks in the last six months when crimes were committed and no drugs were used (2% of unit-weeks) or when drugs were used and no crimes were committed (22% of unit-weeks). The most common combination was for drug-using and crime-committing weeks to coincide (57% of unit-weeks).

The National Treatment Outcome Research Study, a prospective longitudinal study based on 1,070 clients participating in treatment programmes within the United Kingdom, provides some additional information on criminal behaviour. The report of the first year of the research showed that 61 per cent of the sample admitted committing 70,728 offences during the three-month period before intake (including drug offences) (Gossop et al., 1998). Fifty-one per cent of the sample admitted 31,575 non-drug offences during the three-month period before treatment.

Drugs and crime among arrestees

The NEW-ADAM programme surveys collect a wide range of information from among currently active offenders on their drug use and criminal behaviour. It is possible to use this information to identify links between drug use and crime and to identify the target group of high-rate, drug-using offenders referred to in the government's strategy.

The ability of the programme to conduct repeat surveys in the same location on different occasions provides the opportunity to monitor changes in the connection between drugs and crime over time. Information about changes in the proportion of high-rate drug users and high-rate offenders can also be used to evaluate government strategy across locations on a continuing basis.

The following section comprises three chapters that examine the link between drugs and crime. The first examines self-reported illegal income and the various sources of illegal income including drug dealing, social security fraud and property crime. The second looks at acquisitive property time and involvement of arrestees in ten common forms of income-generating crime. The third examines specifically the connection between drug use and crime.

7   Illegal income

Illegal income is a broader concept than acquisitive crime. It covers a variety of ways in which arrestees might obtain income in cash or kind in addition to the normal legal routes of employment or state benefits. There is also a difference between illegal income and property crime (discussed in more detail later). Some property crimes (such as 'joyriding' or 'unsuccessful' property offences) do not generate illegal income, either in cash or in kind. Some forms of illegal income (such as 'undeclared earnings' or 'prostitution') are not normally thought of as property crimes.

The main sources of illegal income among arrestees over the last 12 months are shown in Table 7.1. The most common source of illegal income was property crime, mentioned by about half of all arrestees who reported receiving some illegal income. The second most common source was undeclared earnings, resulting from part-time or full-time work while receiving unemployment or related state benefits. The third most common form of illegal income was generated from drug sales. Very few arrestees said that they generated income from prostitution or from begging. Current NEW-ADAM surveys now ask arrestees specifically about prostitution and prostitution-related offences and it is hoped that this will shed further light on this relationship.

Table 7.1: Sources of illegal income over the last 12 months

	All arrestees		Arrestees reporting some illegal income in the last 12 months	
	n=738		n=301	
	n	%	n	%
Property crime	142	19	142	47
Undeclared earnings	68	9	68	23
Drug dealing/other drug crimes	56	8	56	19
Prostitution	1	-	1	-
Begging	1	-	1	-
Other	33	5	33	11

Notes: Multiple responses possible. Includes only arrestees aged 17–59.

Those arrestees who reported generating illegal income in the last 12 months were asked to estimate the total amount that they had made. Table 7.2 shows that, on average, arrestees reported generating just over £5,000 in illegal income in the last year. This amount varied slightly by area, with arrestees in Liverpool reporting the highest rates (an average of about £9,000 in the last year) and arrestees in Sunderland reporting the lowest rates (an average of about £2,000 in the last year). It is interesting that these two sites had the highest and lowest prevalence rates of heroin and crack/cocaine use respectively.

Overall, there was no significant difference in the mean amounts of illegal income generated among males and females. In two of the sites (South Norwood and Nottingham), males had a slightly higher level of mean illegal income than females and in two sites (Liverpool and Sunderland) females had a slightly higher level than males. There was also no clear correlation between illegal income and age. In the two sites in which it was possible to compare arrestees by ethnic group, whites reported slightly higher illegal incomes than non-whites, although neither was statistically significant.

Table 7.2:   Mean illegal income from all sources over the last 12 months by sex, age and ethnic group, by area

		South Norwood	Liverpool	Nottingham	Sunderland	All 17-59		Total n
		n=143 £	n=209 £	n=204 £	n=182 £	n=738 £		n=738
Sex	Male	6,662	9,144	4,261	2,033	5,602	ns	638
	Female	4,666	9,664	3,734	2,277	5,109		100
Age	17-19	9,529	19,847	4,183	1,113	7,293	ns	163
	20-24	6,624	1,968	5,859	3,811	4,306		182
	25-29	9,457	18,045	3,976	2,568	8,906		157
	30-59	2,689	4,940	2,358	1,566	3,027		236
Ethnic group	White	6,795	8,916	3,972	2,103	5,430	ns	639
	Non-white	6,111	-	5,051	-	6,214		99
All arrestees		6,522	9,214	4,168	2,068	5,535		738

Notes: Includes only arrestees aged 17–59. Mean values include cases with zero illegal income. Includes all amounts as reported with no high-end cut-off.

The next table (Table 7.3) examines differences in the amount of illegal income reported and the use of heroin and crack/cocaine. The table shows a strong correlation between use of these drugs and the amount of illegal income earned. Arrestees who used neither heroin nor crack/cocaine reported about £2,600 of illegal income in the last year. Those who used heroin, but not crack/cocaine, reported just over £3,000 of illegal income and those who used crack/cocaine, but not heroin, reported about £6,500. The highest levels of illegal income were reported by those who used both heroin and crack/cocaine who had mean illegal incomes of almost £13,000 in the last year. The difference in mean illegal income across these groups was statistically significant.

Rates of reported illegal income in the last 12 months increased across the four groups in a similar fashion. Just under one-quarter (23%) of those who used neither heroin nor crack/cocaine (but perhaps other drugs) reported at least some illegal income in the last year. About one-half of heroin users who did not use crack/cocaine and crack/cocaine users who did not use heroin reported some illegal income. However, over three-quarters (79%) of those who used both heroin and crack/cocaine reported illegal incomes.

There was some variation by drug-using group across the four locations. Heroin and crack/cocaine users in Liverpool reported the highest rates of illegal income (almost £16,000 in the last year) and heroin and crack/cocaine users in Sunderland reported the lowest mean levels (about £8,500 in the last year).

Table 7.3: Mean illegal income from all sources over the last 12 months by type of drugs used

	South Norwood	Liverpool	Nottingham	Sunderland	All 17–59	Percentage above zero illegal income	Total number of users
	n=143 £	n=209 £	n=204 £	n=182 £	n=738 £	n=738 £	n=738
Neither heroin nor crack/cocaine use	5,425	4,803	736	943	2,668 ***	23	422
Heroin use – no crack/cocaine use	-	4,252	3,082	2,255	3,024	49	41
Crack/cocaine use – no heroin use	7,430	8,222	5,350	2,895	6,527	47	107
Heroin and crack/cocaine use	11,800	15,771	10,520	8,603	12,719	79	168
All users	6,522	9,214	4,168	2,068	5,535	41	738

Notes: Includes only arrestees aged 17–59. Mean values include cases with zero illegal income. Includes all amounts as reported with no high-end cut-off. * p<.05; ** p<.01; *** p<.001; ns=not significant. T-Test. '-' = too few cases in this category to calculate a mean value.

Table 7.4 shows the total illegal income generated by each drug-using group. This measure is a function of both the total number of arrestees in each group and the mean illegal income generated by them. Hence, the first group who used neither heroin nor crack/cocaine had a fairly large total illegal income (just over £1m), primarily as a result of the large number of arrestees who fell into this group (the mean illegal income of the group was in fact the lowest of the four groups). However, the group using heroin and cocaine generated even higher total illegal incomes, despite the fact that the number of arrestees in this group was much lower. Overall, the heroin and crack/cocaine-using group comprised 23 per cent of the total number of arrestees, yet generated 52 per cent of the total illegal income.

Table 7.4: Mean illegal income from all sources over the last 12 months by type of drugs used

	Total illegal income generated by group £	Percentage total illegal income %	Percentage of total arrestees %	Total n of arrestees n
Neither heroin nor crack/ cocaine use	1,125,945	28	57	422
Heroin use – no crack/ cocaine use	123,970	3	6	41
Crack/cocaine use – no heroin use	698,345	17	15	107
Heroin and crack/ cocaine use	2,136,780	52	23	168
All users	4,085,040	100	101	738

Notes:Includes only arrestees aged 17–59. Mean values include cases with zero illegal income. Includes all amounts as reported with no high-end cut-off. * p<.05; ** p<.01; ***p<.001; ns=not significant. T-Test.

Table 7.5 looks at the relationship between illegal income and the four drug-using groups in a slightly different way. The table aims to estimate the effect of different kinds of drug use on the total illegal income generated by all arrestees. A similar table was compiled in the first developmental stage report. It should be stressed that the information presented so far has told us only that there is a correlation between types of drug use and amount of illegal income generated. It has not told us that drug use caused the illegal income any more than it told us that illegal income caused the drug use (which it might have done). Nevertheless, it is still possible to estimate the contribution of drug use to illegal income under the condition that drug use was the sole cause of the difference in illegal incomes among the four groups. This calculation provides a 'worst case' or 'maximum effect' example of the impact of drug use on illegal behaviour.

Assuming that the use of heroin and crack/cocaine was the sole cause of the differences shown then, in the absence of heroin and crack/cocaine, all groups would have the same mean illegal incomes per year as the first group who used neither of these drugs. As it stands, arrestees generated a combined total illegal income for the whole group in the last 12 months of just over £4 million. If heroin and crack/cocaine users (regardless of whether the drugs were used alone or in combination) had the same illegal incomes as the non-heroin and crack/cocaine users, they would have generated a combined total illegal income in the last 12 months of £1.9 million. The difference is a reduction in illegal income in the order of 52 per cent.

Hence, it could be argued that if all of the difference between the groups in terms of levels of mean illegal income was due solely to the differences in drug use, then, in the absence of this difference, the total illegal income generated by all arrestees would be 52 per cent lower (i.e. a reduction from £4.1 million to £1.9 million). Alternatively, it can be said that if all of the difference between the groups in terms of levels of mean illegal income was due solely to the differences in drug use, the use of heroin and crack/cocaine served to inflate the level of illegal income by just over 100 per cent (i.e. an increase from £1.9 million to £4.1 million). However, it must be understood that this is only a 'what if' calculation and it cannot be assumed that all of the difference between the groups is due to drugs use alone.

Table 7.5: *Estimates of the effect of heroin/crack/cocaine use on illegal income over the last 12 months*

	n	Existing mean illegal income £	Existing total illegal income £	Revised mean illegal income £	Revised total illegal income £	Percentage reduction from existing to revised total illegal income
Neither heroin nor crack/cocaine use	422	2,668	1,125,945	2668	1,125,947	0
Heroin use – no crack/cocaine use	41	3,024	123,970	2668	109,393	12
Crack/cocaine use – no heroin use	107	6,527	698,345	2668	285,489	59
Heroin and crack/cocaine use	168	12,719	2,136,780	2668	448,244	79
Total	738		4,085,040		1,969,073	52

Notes: [1] Total illegal income has been calculated from mean illegal income taken to two decimal points. Hence, the sum shown is slightly different from the sum that can be calculated from the table. Includes only arrestees aged 17–59.

The final table in this chapter looks at changes in mean illegal income over time, by examining the results of the 1997 and 1999 surveys in Nottingham and Sunderland. In Nottingham, there was a slight and non-significant reduction in mean illegal income across the two surveys (an average of £5,528 in 1997 compared with an average of £5,077 in 1999). There were also no significant differences across any of the drug-using groups. In Sunderland, there was a slightly larger reduction in mean illegal income across the two surveys (an average of £3,891 in 1997 compared with an average of £1,786 in 1999). This reduction occurred across three of the four groups and was statistically significant in relation to crack/cocaine users and users of both heroin and crack/cocaine.

It is interesting to speculate on why there was either no change or a reduction in illegal income at a time when the use of the most expensive drugs (heroin and crack/cocaine) appeared to be increasing. One reason for the absence of a more striking increase in illegal activity might be the absence of a similarly striking increase in expenditure on drugs. This was discussed earlier. It was argued that a reduction in the price of heroin and crack/cocaine over the period 1997 to 1999 might have limited the effect of an increase in prevalence on total expenditure on drugs. Another reason is that other factors, which influence illegal income and property crime, might also have changed over this period. While drug use (especially expensive drug use such as heroin and crack/cocaine use) almost certainly has an influence on crime rates, there are many other factors (such as economic and demographic conditions) which also affect crime. During the period 1997 to 1999, for example, property crime rates tended to fall nationally in part because of changing economic conditions.

Table 7.6 :   *Trends in mean illegal income in the last 12 months over time: 1997 and 1999*

	Nottingham			Sunderland		
	1997	1999	Significance of difference	1997	1999	Significance of difference
	n=209	n=204		n=271	n=182	
	£	£		£	£	
Neither heroin nor crack/cocaine use	1,724 (n=140)	682 (n=110)	ns	2,303 (n=219)	918 (n=132)	* (-)
Heroin use – no crack/cocaine use	11,386 (n=11)	3,082 (n=17)	ns	1,705 (n=8)	2,145 (n=11)	ns
Crack/cocaine use – no heroin use	11,779 (n=19)	4,683 (n=18)	ns	5,246 (n=24)	1,000 (n=19)	* (-)
Heroin and crack/cocaine use	14,489 (n=39)	13,967 (n=59)	ns	20,525 (n=20)	8,063 (n=20)	ns
All users	5,528 (n=209)	5,077 (n=204)	ns	3,891 (n=271)	1,786 (n=182)	ns

Notes: This table was compiled from the original force reports and the means for 1999 are slightly different to those presented earlier in this chapter. This is due to the inclusion of all arrestees (rather than just those aged 17–59) and the use of a high-end cut-off (which was not used in the tables shown earlier in this chapter). Mean values include cases with zero illegal income. * p<.05; ** p<.01; ***p<.001; ns=not significant. Chi-squared test: corrected for 2X2 tables, where appropriate. (+) and (-) show the direction of change. The absence of significant finding in relation to some of the apparently large changes in mean illegal income is mainly due to the small number of cases in these categories.

8   Self-reported crime

The current chapter looks at the prevalence and incidence of self-reported acquisitive crime among arrestees. Arrestees were asked whether they had committed each of ten common acquisitive crimes in the whole of their lifetime and over the last 12 months. It should be noted that there is a slight difference between commission of common types of property crime and generation of illegal income (as discussed in the previous chapter). Illegal income might not derive from property crime and property crime might not generate illegal income (especially if the offender is unsuccessful). The main reason for including separate questions on property crime is to identify which crime types arrestees most frequently commit and to determine the connection between the commission of these crime types and drug misuse

The percentage of arrestees who reported committing the ten types of property crime is shown in Table 8.1. The highest lifetime prevalence rates were shown for shoplifting (mentioned by 57% of all arrestees) and handling stolen goods (mentioned by 47% of arrestees). About one-third of arrestees said that they had stolen or taken a motor vehicle (38%) and a similar percentage said that they had stolen items from a motor vehicle (34%). One-fifth (21%) of all arrestees said that they had committed a burglary in a dwelling at some time in their lives and one-quarter (26%) said that they had committed a burglary in another type of building. The distribution of offences was similar over the last 12 months. Just over one-quarter (28%) of arrestees said that they had stolen from a shop and a similar percentage (27%) said that they had handled stolen goods. Relatively few arrestees said that they had committed robbery or had stolen items from the person (e.g. bag snatches). About half of all arrestees interviewed admitted to committing one of the ten acquisitive property crimes in the last 12 months.

There was some variation across the four locations. Arrestees in South Norwood reported higher-than-average or average rates over the last 12 months for vehicle crime, burglary, personal crimes, fraud and drugs supply and lower-than-average rates for shoplifting and handling. Arrestees in Liverpool reported higher-than-average rates for all offences with the exception of burglary in a dwelling. Arrestees in Nottingham reported higher-than-average or average rates for three of the ten offences and lower-than-average rates for seven of the offences. Arrestees in Sunderland reported higher-than-average or average rates for nine of the offence types and lower-than-average rates for one of them (drugs supply).

Table 8.1: Percentage of arrestees reporting each of ten property crimes ever and in the last 12 month

	South Norwood n=143		Liverpool n=209		Nottingham n=204		Sunderland n=182		All 17–59 n=738	
	Ever	Last 12 months	Ever	Last 12 months	Ever	Last 12 months	Ever	Last 12 months	Ever	Last 12 months
Theft of/taking a motor vehicle	36	15	43	13	29	8	46	14	38	12
Theft from a motor vehicle	35	13	38	12	26	5	36	13	34	11
Theft from a shop	48	17	66	35	59	35	52	22	57	28
Burglary dwelling	22	8	19	1	20	5	23	8	21	5
Burglary non-dwelling	27	8	32	9	16	5	29	9	26	8
Robbery	11	2	12	4	7	1	10	2	10	2
Theft person	4	1	8	2	4	1	6	1	5	1
Fraud/deception	29	13	23	13	17	8	21	12	22	11
Handling	43	22	53	30	38	24	53	32	47	27
Drugs supply	22	14	28	14	21	11	15	8	22	12
Any offence	74	42	85	56	70	51	80	47	78	50

Notes: Includes only arrestees aged 17–59.

The second table (Table 8.2) provides a breakdown of the prevalence of offending by sex, age and ethnic group. Overall, females had a higher prevalence rate than males of one or more of the selected property crimes (60% females compared with 48% males)(statistically significant). This result is notable as it is consistent with the earlier finding that females had higher prevalence rates than males of use of opiates and crack/cocaine. In relation to four of the ten offences (theft from a motor vehicle, shoplifting, robbery and theft from the person), the 12-month prevalence rates were higher for females than for males. Males had higher prevalence rates than females in relation to five of the offences, and the percentage was the same in relation to one of the offences.

There was very little difference among younger (17-to-24-year-old) and older (25-to-59-year-old) arrestees in terms of the prevalence of offending. In most cases the prevalence rate of the two groups was within one or two percentage points. White arrestees had slightly higher prevalence rates than non-white arrestees for shoplifting and for the commission of one or more offences (statistically significant). However, for most of the offence types there was almost no difference in the percentages.

Table 8.2: Percentage of arrestees reporting each of ten property crimes in the last 12 months by age, sex and ethnic group status

	Sex		Age		Ethnic Group		All 17–59
	Male	Female	17–24	25–59	White	Non-white	
Theft of/taking a motor vehicle	13	10	12	13	13	12	12
Theft from a motor vehicle	10	13	12	10	11	11	11
Theft from a shop	28	31	29	28	29	25	28
Burglary dwelling	6	5	6	6	6	5	5
Burglary non-dwelling	8	8	7	9	8	6	8
Robbery	2	5	1	3	2	4	2
Theft person	1	3	1	1	1	2	1
Fraud/deception	12	8	11	12	11	10	11
Handling	28	26	27	28	27	29	27
Drugs supply	12	10	12	11	12	10	12
Any offence	48	60 *	53	47	52	35 **	50

Notes: Includes only arrestees aged 17–59. * $p<.05$; ** $p<.01$; *** $p<.001$; ns=not significant. Chi-squared test: corrected for 2X2 tables, where appropriate.

Table 8.3 shows the proportion of arrestees reporting each offence type by involvement in drug misuse. In relation to most of the ten offence types, users of heroin and crack/cocaine were significantly more likely than non-users to report committing them. In most cases, users of both heroin and crack/cocaine were more likely than users of heroin alone or crack/cocaine alone to report committing the offences. Users of both heroin and cocaine were more than five times more likely to report committing robbery and more than four times more likely to report shoplifting than arrestees who did not use these drugs. They were also three times more likely to report residential and non-residential burglary.

Table 8.3: Percentage of arrestees reporting each of ten property crimes in the last 12 months by type of drugs used

	Neither heroin nor crack/cocaine n=424		Heroin n=41		Crack/cocaine n=107		Heroin and crack/cocaine n=168	
	%	n	%	n	%	n	%	n
Theft of/taking a motor vehicle	8	34	10	4	20	21	19 ***	32
Theft from a motor vehicle	7	31	12	5	11	12	18 **	30
Theft from a shop	15	64	42	17	19	20	65 ***	109
Burglary dwelling	4	17	15	6	-	-	11	18
Burglary non-dwelling	5	22	5	2	8	9	15 ***	25
Robbery	1	3	5	2	5	5	5 **	8
Theft person	1	3	-	-	3	3	2	4
Fraud/deception	7	29	7	3	16	17	20 ***	34
Handling	18	78	39	16	33	35	44 ***	73
Drugs supply	6	24	10	4	21	22	22 ***	37
Any offence	33	140	61	25	53	57	87 ***	146

Notes: Includes all arrestees. * $p < .05$; ** $p < .01$; *** $p < .001$; ns=not significant. Chi-squared test: corrected for 2X2 tables, where appropriate. '-' zero cases.

The next table (Table 8.4) shows the total number of acquisitive crimes committed in the last 12 months. This number has been calculated by adding together the reported number of offences for each of the ten crime types mentioned above. The table is also broken down by sex, age and ethnic group status. The table shows that there was little difference in the number of crimes reported by males and females. In two of the locations males reported slightly higher numbers of property crime than females and in the other two sites females reported either exactly the same number or a slightly higher number. None of the differences was statistically significant. Younger arrestees (aged under 25) tended to report higher mean numbers of property crimes than older arrestees (aged 25 to 59). However, this relationship was significant only among arrestees in South Norwood. It was not possible to compare offence rates by ethnic group in two of the four sites, as the numbers were too low. In the remaining two sites (South Norwood and Nottingham), white arrestees reported slightly higher numbers of offences than non-white arrestees (neither difference was statistically significant).

Table 8.4: Mean number of selected property offences committed in the last 12 months by sex, age and ethnic group

	South Norwood	Liverpool	Nottingham	Sunderland	All 17–59	Total number
	n=143	n=209	n=204	n=182	n=738	n=738 [1]
Sex						
Male	59	92	126	109	98	625
Female	75	92	92	76	86	95
Age						
17–19	122 *	113	156	155	141	161
20–24	85	55	129	125	98	178
25–29	31	135	94	69	83	151
30–59	36	90	96	67	73	230
Ethnic group						
White	71	93	126	106	103	623
Non-white	42	-	92	-	59	97
All arrestees	60	92	120	104	97	720[1]

Notes: Includes only arrestees aged 17–59. Mean values includes cases with zero reported offences. The total number of offences reported in each offence type were cut-off at the highest levels. * p<.05; ** p<.01; ***p<.001; ns=not significant. T-Test. '-' = too few cases in this category to calculate a mean value. [1] 18 cases missing.

Table 8.5 shows the mean number of offences committed among users of different types of drugs. The table shows that arrestees who reported using heroin or crack/cocaine in the last 12 months reported a higher mean number of offences than non-users. Overall, the mean number of offences reported among users of drugs other than heroin and crack/cocaine was 52 in the last 12 months. Users of heroin without crack/cocaine and users of crack/cocaine without heroin had a mean offence rate of twice that number. Arrestees who used both heroin and crack/cocaine had mean offence rates over four times the rate of non-heroin and crack/cocaine users. In all areas, the difference in means among all four groups shown in the table was statistically significant.

Table 8.5:   *Mean number of selected property offences committed in the last 12 months by type of drugs used*

	South n=139	Liverpool n=199	Nottingham n=204	Sunderland n=178	All 17–59 n=720	Total n=720 [1]
Neither heroin nor crack/cocaine use	23***	19***	72***	71 *	52***	418
Heroin use – no crack/cocaine use	-	102	98	172	114	41
Crack/cocaine use – no heroin use	105	101	101	109	104	103
Heroin and crack/cocaine use	192	186	221	239	206	158
Total	60	92	120	104	97	720

Notes:Includes only arrestees aged 17–59. Mean values include cases with zero reported offences. The total number of offences reported in each offence type were cut-off at the highest levels. * $p<.05$; ** $p<.01$; ***$p<.001$; ns=not significant. T-Test. '-' = too few cases in this category to calculate a mean value. [1] 18 cases missing.

The extent of involvement in criminal behaviour among users of heroin and cocaine is a key component of the current government's drugs strategy. It was mentioned earlier that one of the aims of the second key objective was to reduce levels of repeat offending among drug-misusing offenders. It would be possible to operationalise this objective to refer to arrestees. The phrase 'drug-misusing offenders' could refer to arrestees who admitted using heroin or crack/cocaine in the last 12 months. The phrase 'repeat offending' could refer to arrestees who admitted a high-rate of offending over the last 12 months or last month. 'High-rate' might be interpreted as 20 or more offences a month.

It is possible to determine from the current data the proportion of arrestees that would be identified from definitions of this kind. The following table shows the percentage of arrestees who admitted an average of 20 or more offences per month over the last year and who reported using heroin or crack/cocaine. Over two-thirds of the highest-rate offenders (20 offences a month or more) reported using heroin or crack/cocaine. Overall, nine per cent of the total sample of arrestees could be classified as high-rate offenders and users of heroin or crack/cocaine. This nine per cent of arrestees was responsible for one-third (34%) of all illegal income and over one-half (52%) of all reported offences.

Table 8.6: *Percentage of arrestees who used heroin or crack/cocaine in the last 12 months by total number of selected property offences committed*

	No offences	Less than 20 offences a month on average	20 offences or more a month on average	Total number of users
	n=371	n=250	n=99	n=720
Neither heroin nor crack/cocaine use	76	41	32	58
Heroin or crack/cocaine use	24	59	68	42
Total	100	100	100	100

Notes: Includes only arrestees aged 17–59. The total number of offences reported in each offence type were cut-off at the highest levels. * p<.05; ** p<.01; ***p<.001; ns=not significant. Chi-squared test: corrected for 2X2 tables, where appropriate. 18 cases missing.

Overall, the chapter has shown that arrestees reported a high number of offences in the last 12 months. The prevalence of shoplifting was particularly high (the majority of arrestees admitted this offence). However, about one-third of all arrestees had committed a vehicle crime and about one-quarter had committed a burglary. There were few clear differences in rate of offending and arrestee characteristics, although younger arrestees tended to report higher rates of offending than older arrestees. The clearest difference among arrestees and offending rates occurred in relation to drug use. Arrestees who used either heroin or crack/cocaine reported significantly higher number of offences than those who did not. The highest rate offenders were those who used both heroin and crack/cocaine.

The government's drugs strategy is based on the principle that drugs and crime are connected and that communities can be made safer places more generally if drug use and associated problems could be reduced. The current chapter brings together some of the findings of the previous two chapters and examines the relationship between drugs and crime. The first part of the chapter looks in more detail at the statistical association between measures of drug use and measures of crime. The second part considers the causal connection between the two more directly and examines what arrestees say about the link between their own drug use and crime.

Table 9.1 compares a number of measures of drug use and crime. The first comparison is the number of positive tests for drugs (excluding alcohol) and four measures of criminal behaviour. The table shows a statistically significant correlation across all four measures. Arrestees who tested positive for three or more drugs reported on average three times as many offences as those who had zero positive tests. They reported committing more than twice as many offence types and eight times the illegal income. They also reported more than twice as many arrests in the last 12 months.

The second measure of drug use is expenditure on drugs in the last seven days. The table shows that there is also a statistically significant association between this measure of drug misuse and each of the measures of criminal behaviour. In relation to three of the four measures, there is a clear linear progression, with the various measures of involvement in crime increasing as the measure of drug misuse increases. Arrestees who reported spending £100 or more on drugs reported ten times the number of offences as those who reported no expenditure on drugs. They also reported four times the mean number of offence types committed in the last 12 months, eight times the mean illegal income and almost twice as many arrests.

The third measure shown in the table is the number of self-reported drug types used in the last 12 months. There is also a clear linear relationship between this measure of drug use and most of the measures of criminal behaviour (all correlations were statistically significant). Arrestees who reported using three or more drug types in the last 12 months, reported more offences, more offence types, greater illegal income and more arrests than those who reported using no drug types.

There is little doubt that drug use and crime are statistically correlated among the current samples of arrestees. There is clear evidence that as drug use increases involvement in criminal behaviour tends to increase. However, it cannot be assumed from this that drug use causes offending or that offending causes drug use. Attempts to determine a causal relationship between drug use and crime are beyond the scope of the current report. However, there is some additional evidence that can be drawn upon to estimate the likelihood that one of these variables causes the other.

Table 9.1: Various measures of involvement in drug use by various measures of involvement in crime

	Mean number of offences committed in the last 12 months n=740	Mean number of offence types committed out of 10 property crime types in the last 12 months n=740	Mean illegal income in the last 12 months n=740 £	Mean number of arrests excluding current arrest in the last 12 months n=740
Number of positive tests excluding alcohol n=506				
0	48 ***	0.7 ***	1,645 **	1.7 *
1	114	1.3	3,575	3.9
2	125	1.5	9,231	2.8
3 or more	171	2.2	13,267	4.2
Expenditure on drugs in the last 7 days n=740				
0	28 ***	0.5 ***	2,140 ***	2.0 *
£1–£99	80	1.3	1,633	2.7
£100 or more	246	2.3	16,881	3.8
Number of drug types used out of 19 self-report categories (excluding alcohol and tobacco) in the last 12 months n=740				
0	10 ***	0.2 ***	2211 ***	1.0 ***
1	26	0.5	1100	1.6
2	95	1.5	3481	4.0
3 or more	176	1.9	9671	3.7

Notes: All ages. * p<.05; ** p<.01; ***p<.001 ns=not significant. : T-Test.

All arrestees who reported using at least one drug in the last 12 months and at least one offence were asked whether they thought that their drug use and crime were connected. The results are shown in Table 9.2.

Just over 40 per cent (42%) of arrestees said that they thought that their drug use and crime were connected. This percentage varied slightly across survey locations. About one-third (30%) of arrestees in Sunderland thought that their drug use and crime were connected (the lowest percentage) compared with almost half (49%) of arrestees in Nottingham (the highest percentage). Those arrestees who said that they thought that there was a connection were asked about the nature of the association. The majority of arrestees (70%) said that the two were connected because they needed money to buy drugs. The remainder thought that drugs affected their judgement which thereby caused crime or that they used the money from crime to buy drugs.

Hence, arrestees' perceptions provide some additional information on the association between drugs and crime. Almost half of offenders believed that their drug use and crime were connected and those that did so most frequently believed that drug use caused crime because it generated a need for money to buy drugs or because drug use affected their judgement in some way. Not many arrestees thought that crime caused drug use.

Table 9.2: *Perceived connection between drug use and crime (drug users in the last 12 months only)*

	South Norwood	Liverpool	Nottingham	Sunderland	All users
In the last 12 months, do you think that your drug use was in any way connected to your offending?					
Yes	34	48	49	30	42
No	66	52	51	70	58
Total %	100	100	100	100	100
Total n [1]	95	167	160	142	564
(If yes) In what way do you think your drug use was connected to your offending? [3]					
Affect of drugs on judgement	22	14	22	56	25
Need for money to buy drugs	44	85	79	44	70
Money from crime used to buy drugs	13	11	11	7	11
Other connection	19	10	10	14	12
Total n [2]	32	80	79	43	234

Notes: Includes arrestees of all ages. [1] Includes only drug users in the last 12 months. [2] Includes only arrestees who thought that there was a connection between drug use and crime. [3] Multiple responses possible.

The final table in this section looks at the relationship between cannabis and opioid use and crime.

Table 9.3 shows the association between cannabis use in the last 12 months and various measures of crime. The table shows that cannabis users are associated with slightly higher levels of criminal involvement than users of no drugs. The mean number of offences and mean number of types of offences are each slightly higher among cannabis users than non-users (both differences are statistically significant). However, the other two measures (mean illegal income and mean number of arrests) do not show such a clear relationship. The table also shows that users of drugs apart from heroin or crack/cocaine who include cannabis in their repertoire of drugs tend to have slightly higher mean values of criminal involvement than those who do not (but only one of the comparisons reached statistical significance). Users of heroin and/or crack/cocaine who also use cannabis also generate slightly higher mean values in terms of the measures of criminal involvement. However, none of these differences was statistically significant. Hence, there is some suggestion from these findings that cannabis use is associated with a slight inflation of criminal involvement. However, the fact that only some of the associations reached statistical significance needs to be borne in mind when evaluating these results.

The second part of the table shows the association between opioid use in the last 12 months and the four measures of crime. Opioids are 'opiate like' substances which are sometimes used as substitutes for heroin and include methadone, diconal, DF118s and temgesic. It is possible that arrestees who use heroin substitutes are more heavily involved in drug use and more likely to be involved in criminal behaviour. The table shows that there is some evidence that users of opioids do report higher levels of criminal involvement than non users. The first comparison (users of opioids alone with non drug users) could not be conducted because there were no cases in which arrestees used only opioids and no other drugs. The second comparison looks at users of other drugs apart from heroin and cocaine. Users of other drugs apart from heroin and cocaine who also use opioids were significantly more likely to report higher levels of criminal involvement on each of the four measures of crime. The third comparison examines the additional effect of opioids on heroin and crack/cocaine users. The table shows that heroin and/or crack/cocaine users who also used opioids were more involved in crime on each of the four measures. However, only two of the differences were statistically significant.

Table 9.3: Use of cannabis and opioids in combination with other drugs by various measures of involvement in crime

n=740	Mean number of offences committed in the last 12 months crime types in	Mean number of offence types committed out of 10 property the last 12 months n=740	Mean illegal income in the last 12 months n=740 months	Mean number of arrests excluding current arrest in the last 12 n=740
Cannabis comparison				
No drugs				
Without cannabis	10 *	0.2**	2,211	1.0
With cannabis	29	0.6*	1,198	1.6
Other drugs apart from heroin or crack/cocaine				
Without cannabis	69	0.8*	1,426	2.2
With cannabis	161	1.8	5,843	4.6
Heroin and/or crack/cocaine				
Without cannabis	104	1.8	8,094	2.3
With cannabis	166	1.8	9,559	3.6
Opioid comparison [1]				
No drugs				
Without opioids	10	0.2	2,211	1.0
With opioids	-	-	-	-
Other drugs apart from h or c				
Without opioids	66***	1.0 ***	1,610 ***	2.7 ***
With opioids	332	2.7	22,172	4.8
Heroin and/or crack/cocaine				
Without opioids	120 **	1.5 **	6,855	3.1
With opioids	200	2.1	11,971	3.8

Notes: [1] 'Opioids' = synthetic heroin substitutes [excluding heroin]. These include methadone, diconal, DF118s and temgesic. '-' no cases'.

Overall, the chapter has shown that there are a number of strong correlations between certain kinds of drug use and criminal behaviour. While not all of the associations found were statistically significant, the findings in most cases tended to be in the direction of showing that arrestees who used drugs, especially heroin and/or crack/cocaine, were more likely than those who did not use drugs to be involved in criminal behaviour and were also more likely to be involved in higher rates of criminal behaviour.

Conclusion on drugs and crime

The results of the second developmental stage of the NEW-ADAM programme have provided some additional evidence on the nature of the relationship between drug use and crime. The results have shown that drug users have higher levels of illegal income and higher rates of self-reported crime than non users. The results also have shown a strong correlation between a wide range of measures of drug use and a wide range of measures of crime. Almost half of arrestees believe that there is a connection between their own drug use and offending.

The research findings so far suggest that drug use (especially heroin and crack/cocaine use) is associated with higher levels of both prevalence (the proportion of the population involved) and incidence (the rate of offending of those involved) of offending.

Establishing the precise nature of this connection and the extent to which the drug use causes crime is beyond the scope of the current report. However, it is hoped that results of further NEW-ADAM surveys and (in particular) the analysis of the forthcoming trend data will help throw additional light on the problem.

Part Three: Health and treatment

Key Performance Target Three

The third key objective of the drugs stategy is to enable people with drugs problems to overcome them and live healthy and crime-free lives. In particular, it aims to reduce the number of people who inject drugs and to reduce the number of injectors who share needles. The main method of achieving this is to increase the provision of treatment services and to increase the use of these services. The strategy also refers to the problem of Hepatitis B and proposes methods for reducing it.

The effectiveness of treatment

One of the key elements of the government's strategy is to increase the availability of treatment services to drug misusers. The policy is based on a number of assumptions, including the belief that users want treatment services and would use them if they were available. It is also based on the assumption that treatment services are effective in achieving health-related and other objectives. The NEW-ADAM surveys include a number of questions on health and treatment and the following sections attempt to assess the unmet need for treatment among arrestees. However, before doing this, it might be useful to review briefly some of the recent research which has investigated whether drug treatment is effective in helping users to reduce their drug use or abstain from drugs and whether (as a result) it is effective in reducing their criminal behaviour and other drug-related problems.

Reducing drug use

One of the largest treatment evaluation studies in this country is the National Treatment Outcome Research Study (NTORS) (Gossop et al., 1998). The study is a prospective, longitudinal study based on a cohort of 1,075 clients of four representative treatment modalities (specialist inpatient treatment, rehabilitation programmes, methadone maintenance and methadone reduction programmes). Outcome data are available for the first year of the research for 753 of the 1,075 clients. The evaluation showed reductions from intake to the one year follow-up in various kinds of drug-using behaviours, including frequency of drug use, abstinence, and injecting behaviour. In addition, the clients experienced various kinds of health improvements, including improvements in physical and mental health.

One of the largest studies on the effectiveness of referral schemes (referring offenders passing through the criminal justice system into treatment) is currently being conducted by researchers at South Bank University. The most recent report in this series summarises the results of work done so far (Edmunds et al., 1999). The main part of the study covers arrest referral schemes and referrals as part of a probation order. An additional small group of respondents who had contact with prison-based criminal justice workers was also included. The results section of the report focuses on 205 individuals who were contacted through arrest referral schemes or referred through a probation office (excluding respondents interviewed as part of a separate prison sample). Three-quarters of offenders (77%) who were contacted by criminal justice drug workers were referred to some kind of treatment service. Fifty-one per cent of offenders attended the service. The main forms of treatment offered were counselling, advice and information, or a drugs prescription. After a period of between six and nine months following initial contact, 52 per cent were still in treatment, 22 per cent had completed treatment, and 27 per cent had left of their own accord, were asked to leave, or left for other reasons.

The main impact evaluation is based on all offenders offered help (rather than those who took up treatment services) who were not in prison at the time the interview was conducted (n=178). The study found that the proportion of offenders reporting using drugs in the 30-day period before contact and the 30-day period before interview in most instances declined (with the exceptions of prescribed methadone and alcohol). The largest reductions were in crack/cocaine use. The prevalence of injecting also fell (from 69% to 47%), as did the median weekly expenditure on drugs.

Parker and Kirby (1996) evaluated a large methadone maintenance programme in Merseyside by comparing changes in the methadone sample and a community sample not in treatment (but currently taking part in a local needle-exchange scheme). They found that the mean number of illegal (non-prescribed) drugs used in the last four weeks was 1.8 for the treatment sample and 3.1 for the community sample. Over half of the treatment sample (56%) had used heroin in the past four weeks compared with over 90 per cent (91%) of the community sample. Seventy-one per cent of the treatment sample said that they thought they were now using 'less' illegal drugs than before treatment and 22 per cent said that they had 'completely stopped' illegal drug use.

Reducing crime

The ostensible aim of drug treatment programmes is typically to encourage drug users to reduce their drug use or abstain from drug use. It is less typically an aim to provide treatment in order to reduce crime. However, it is logically possible (assuming that drug use and crime are connected) that programmes which reduce drug use also reduce criminal behaviour.

The NTORS national study of clients in treatment programmes mentioned earlier also considered the impact of treatment on criminal behaviour (Gossop et al., 1998). The authors found that the rates of criminal behaviour at intake were substantially lower at the one-year follow-up. There were notable reductions in both drug offences and non-drug acquisitive crimes among clients of both the residential and the community-based programmes. Specifically, they found a 60 per cent reduction in the prevalence of shoplifting among the residential clients and a 70 per cent reduction among the community clients. The prevalence of burglary reduced by 87 per cent and 70 per cent respectively among clients of the residential and community treatment programmes.

Edmunds et al. (1999), in their study of referral schemes, also discussed the effect of the programmes on offending. They measured offending by asking respondents whether they had committed a range of crimes in the month before contact with the criminal justice drug worker and in the month before interview. The results presented focus on the commission of property crimes. They found that 44 per cent of the sample reported no property crimes in the month before interview (they had ceased offending) and 17 per cent said that they had committed fewer property offences. Ten per cent said that they committed the same amount and six per cent said that they had increased. Twenty-three per cent had committed only non-property crimes.

A study by Bennett and Wright (1986) of drug users currently receiving a prescription for heroin substitutes from a drug clinic (2 groups) or a general (1 group) or private practitioner (1 group) examined (amongst other things) the possible effect of the programmes on criminal behaviour. In the year before receiving a prescription, between 48 per cent and 100 per cent of users (depending on the group) reported committing at least one non-drug crime. In the first year of receiving a prescription, between nine per cent and 48 per cent of users reported committing at least one non-drug crime. The prevalence of offending reduced across users in each of the four treatment groups.

Jarvis and Parker's (1989) study of heroin users attending a drug dependency clinic in London or currently serving a term of imprisonment showed that they tended to commit fewer crimes when in treatment than when not in treatment. Over the last six months, 72 per cent of the drug users said that they had committed a crime when they were not in treatment, compared with 36 per cent who said that they had committed a crime when they were in treatment.

Health and treatment needs among arrestees

The research on the effectiveness of treatment shows quite strongly that treatment can have some impact on drug use and crime – at least in the short term. It will be interesting to see the results of the longer-term follow-ups of the NTORS research which will be able to comment on the longer-term impact of treatment. However, treatment programmes can only be effective among those drug users who enter treatment and who remain in treatment for at least some of the duration of the programme. Developments in referral schemes and drug treatment and testing orders provide one way of tackling the unmet need for treatment among drug users. The NEW-ADAM programme surveys can help monitor the spread and changes in use of treatment services over time and the extent of the unmet need for treatment. It will also be possible to examine, at an aggregate level, changes in the prevalence of exposure to treatment and changes in the prevalence of problems relating to drug misuse.

The following section comprises three chapters that look at aspects of health and treatment in relation to arrestees. The first chapter looks at health and the extent to which arrestees are currently under treatment for health problems. It also looks at drug dependence and the extent to which arrestees are currently dependent on drugs and the type of drugs. The second considers injecting behaviour and the extent to which injectors share syringes. The third looks at use of treatment in the past and in the present and estimates the unmet need for treatment services among currently active offenders.

10   **Health and drug dependence**

One of the many problems associated with drug misuse is drug dependence. In a medical sense, dependence refers to the development of a tolerance for a drug which results in withdrawal symptoms when the drug is removed. In the current chapter, the word 'dependence' is used slightly more broadly to include psychological as well as physical dependence. Specifically, arrestees were asked whether they felt that they needed the drug or felt bad or ill when they did not have it.

Drug dependence is a problem in its own right because it serves to perpetuate drug use and the problems associated with it. In fact, dependent users are commonly defined as problem drug users and it is widely believed that such users are the main sources of the common problem behaviours associated with drug misuse, such as health problems and crime.

The extent of drug dependence was investigated by asking arrestees, who admitted taking any of the 19 drug types mentioned earlier, whether they thought they were currently dependent on the drug.

Table 10.1 :   **Current dependency on selected drugs**

Percentages

	South Norwood	Liverpool	Nottingham	Sunderland	All arrestees
Amphetamines	0	1	3	7	3
Cannabis	10	12	10	7	10
Cocaine	4	6	1	0	3
Crack	6	11	5	1	6
Ecstasy	1	0	0	1	-
Heroin	9	32	23	6	19
LSD	0	0	0	1	-
Magic mushrooms	0	0	0	0	0
Methadone	3	12	3	2	5
Steroids	0	1	0	0	-
Temazepam	3	1	2	2	2
Diazepam	1	1	1	5	2
Other tranquillisers	0	0	2	2	1
Barbiturates	0	0	0	1	-
Diconal	0	0	0	1	-
DF118s	0	2	1	2	2
Temgesic	0	1	0	1	-
Amyl nitrite	0	1	0	0	-
Solvents	0	0	0	0	0
Tobacco	50	75	72	59	65
Alcohol	12	6	6	10	8
Any drug	21	45	36	24	33

Note: '-' less than 0.5%. Figures for dependency on any drug exclude alcohol and tobacco.

Table 10.1 shows that one-third (33%) of arrestees said that they were dependent on at least one drug at the time of the interview. This percentage varied slightly across the four locations with Liverpool showing the highest rate (45% currently dependent) and South Norwood the lowest rate (21% currently dependent). The three drugs most frequently associated with dependence were tobacco (65% dependent), heroin (19% dependent) and cannabis (10% dependent). Dependence on heroin was highest in Liverpool (almost one-third of arrestees said that they were currently dependent upon it) and lowest in Sunderland (6% said they were dependent). The drugs least frequently associated with dependence were magic mushrooms and solvents (0%) and temgesic and amyl nitrite (less than 1%).

Table 10.2: Current dependency by number of drugs

Percentages

Number of drug types currently dependent on out of 19 selected drug types	South Norwood	Liverpool	Nottingham	Sunderland	All arrestees
0	79	55	64	76	67
1	10	25	26	17	20
2	6	12	7	4	8
3	4	6	3	2	4
4	1	1	1	1	1
5	0	1	0	1	1
6	0	0	0	0	0
7	0	1	0	0	0
Total	100	100	100	100	100

[1] Excluding tobacco and alcohol. '-' less than 0.5%.

Table 10.2 shows the number of drugs on which arrestees said that they were currently dependent. The table is based on the 19 drug types shown in Table 10.1. Twenty per cent of arrestees were dependent on one drug type and 14 per cent were dependent on two or more drug types. In other words, 14 per cent of the sample were poly-drug or multiple-drug dependent. The highest percentage of poly-drug dependency was in Liverpool, where 21 per cent of all arrestees said that they were dependent on two or more drugs.

Changes in the prevalence of dependency over time are shown in Table 10.3. In Nottingham, during the period 1997 to 1999, the percentage of arrestees who said that they were currently dependent on heroin increased from 12 per cent to 23 per cent (statistically significant), whereas the percentage who said that they were currently dependent on alcohol decreased (also significant). In Sunderland, there was an increase in the percentage of arrestees who said that they were dependent on heroin (this relationship was not statistically significant). At the same time, there was a notable reduction in the percentage of arrestees who said that they were dependent on alcohol (which was statistically significant). Taken together, these two findings concerning changing patterns of dependency in Sunderland echo earlier findings on the worsening drug situation in this area.

The reduction in the use of alcohol across the two sites lends some support to the evidence collected to date from the NEW-ADAM surveys of a negative association between alcohol use and drug use. This association has been found at both the area level and the individual level. The current finding points very tentatively to the possibility that the association might also hold over time, whereby increases in drug use are associated with decreases in alcohol use, and vice versa.

Table 10.3 : Current dependency on selected drugs over time: 1997 and 1999

Percentages

	Nottingham			Sunderland		
	1997	1999	Significance of difference	1997	1999	Significance of difference
	n=209	n=204		n=271	n=182	
Amphetamines	4	4	ns	4	7	ns
Cannabis	11	10	ns	8	7	ns
Cocaine	1	1	ns	0	0	ns
Crack	4	5	ns	0	1	ns
Ecstasy	0	0	ns	1	0	ns
Heroin	12	23	** (+)	4	6	ns
LSD	1	0	ns	0	1	ns
Magic mushrooms	0	0	ns	0	0	ns
Methadone	4	3	ns	2	2	ns
Temazepam	2	2	ns	3	2	ns
Diazepam	3	1	ns	4	5	ns
Other tranquillisers	3	2	ns	3	2	ns
Barbiturates	1	0	ns	0	1	ns
Diconal	1	0	ns	0	1	ns
DF118s	1	1	ns	0	2	ns
Temgesic	1	0	ns	2	1	ns
Amyl nitrite	0	0	ns	0	0	ns
Solvents	1	0	ns	0	0	ns
Tobacco	69	72	ns	66	59	ns
Alcohol	14	6	* (-)	19	10	* (-)

Notes: *= $p<.05$; **= $p<.01$; ***=$p<.001$ Chi-squared test: corrected for 2X2 tables, where appropriate. (+) and (-) show the direction of change.

Drug dependent arrestees are at a greater risk of poor health and disease than non-drug dependent arrestees. Just over one per cent of all arrestees thought that they were HIV positive (1% among heroin and/or crack/cocaine users) and about seven per cent said that they mixed with people who were HIV positive (12% among heroin and/or crack/cocaine users). One per cent of the sample said that they currently had hepatitis (2% among heroin and/or crack/cocaine users) and about eight per cent said that they mixed with people who had hepatitis (17% among heroin and/or crack/cocaine users).

Arrestees were also asked if they were currently using drugs prescribed by a doctor or drugs purchased over-the-counter in the treatment of health problems. About one-quarter of arrestees (24%) said that they had recently (in the last 3 days) taken drugs prescribed by a doctor for a health problem (including the treatment of addiction) and about 12 per cent said that they had consumed drugs purchased over-the-counter.

Table 10.4: Percentage of arrestees reporting being under prescription from a doctor or buying drugs over-the-counter by type of illness

Illness		Arrestees who were prescribed a drug by a doctor n=174		Arrestees who purchased drugs over-the-counter n=89	
		n	%	n	%
Addiction/drug related	heroin/other	49	28	3	3
Psychological/psychiatric	depression	32	18	6	7
	insomnia	6	3	1	1
	anxiety	8	5	1	1
	other	1	1	0	0
Infection/inflammation	chest	2	1	1	1
	cough/cold/flu	3	2	6	7
	other	4	2	0	0
Pain	recent surgery	2	1	1	1
	headache/migraine	4	2	25	28
	back	11	6	2	2
	stomach	3	2	3	3
	teeth/mouth	4	2	10	11
	arthritis	5	3	2	2
	other	2	1	4	5
Allergies	hay fever	3	2	3	3
	asthma	19	11	4	5
	other	1	1	0	0
Conditions/abnormalities	heart/lungs	5	3	2	2
	kidneys/bladder/bowels	2	1	1	1
	epilepsy	3	2	1	1
	diabetes	2	1	0	0
	hypertension	1	1	0	0
	other	0	0	3	3
Injury	back	1	1	0	0
	head	3	2	0	0
	other	5	3	1	1
Other/unspecified		11	6	9	10

Notes: Includes all arrestees. Multiple responses possible.

The kinds of health problems experienced by arrestees are listed in Table 10.4. The most common health problem associated with drugs prescribed by a doctor concerned addiction.

About one-quarter of all arrestees currently under prescription were receiving drugs for the treatment of addiction (typically heroin addiction). This category included receiving methadone for the treatment of addiction. Almost one-fifth of arrestees currently receiving prescribed drugs were suffering from depression (18%). A further five per cent of arrestees under prescription were suffering from anxiety attacks. Other common health problems included back pain (6% of those receiving a prescription) and asthma (experienced by 11% of arrestees currently on a prescription). A notable number of arrestees had serious health conditions affecting the heart or lungs or other major organs and another group was carrying a recent injury to their back, face or head (the latter was sometimes associated with a recent assault).

Slightly over a quarter of all arrestees who had consumed over-the-counter drugs in the last three days were suffering from headaches or migraine. Eleven per cent had toothache or pains in the mouth. Seven per cent of arrestees using over-the-counter drugs were suffering from depression and five per cent had asthma.

It is very likely that the prevalence of current illness among arrestees is higher than would be found in a comparable sub-group of the general population. Some of these illnesses are clearly drug-related. Treatment for drug addiction is obviously drug-related. However, some of the other illnesses such as asthma, headaches and stomach problems might also be a product of drug-taking (especially heroin misuse). It is possible also that some of the cases of depression or anxiety are drug-related.

11   Injecting behaviour

One of the aims of the drugs strategy is to reduce the number of drug users who inject and to reduce the number of injectors who share. Injection is potentially the most harmful way of administering drugs. It carries various kinds of health risk to the user (such as infection, abscesses, the risk of overdose) and various kinds of health risks to others (such as cross infection when equipment is shared and health problems relating to disposal of used syringes). Injection also might serve to escalate addiction and drug use as a result of the potential for increased perceived benefits on the part of the drug user and the possibility of consuming larger amounts of the drug than normal and more quickly.

The following table (Table 11.1) shows the prevalence of injection among all arrestees in the four locations. About one-quarter (23%) of arrestees said that they had injected an illegal drug at some time in the lives and about one-fifth (18%) said that they had done so in the last 12 months. The percentage of arrestees who had injected in the last 12 months varied across sites. Almost a quarter of arrestees in Liverpool and Nottingham (24% in each site) said that they had recently injected a drug, compared with 14 per cent in Sunderland and six per cent in South Norwood. The most frequently injected drug in the last 12 months was heroin (14% of arrestees had injected it) followed by cocaine (8%) and amphetamines (8%). Heroin was the most frequently injected drug across three of the four sites, whereas amphetamine was the most frequently injected drug in one of the four sites (Sunderland).

Table 11.1: Percentage of all arrestees who reported injecting selected drugs over various periods of time

	South Norwood n=145		Liverpool n=209		Nottingham n=204		Sunderland n=182		All arrestees n=740	
	Ever	Last 12 months	Ever	Last 12 months	Ever	Last 12 months	Ever	Last 12 months	Ever	Last 12 months
Heroin	6	6	28	23	22	16	11	7	18	14
Methadone	1	1	7	4	1	0	1	0	3	1
Cocaine	5	3	24	18	8	6	3	1	11	8
Amphetamines	4	2	12	7	18	12	12	8	12	8
Other drug	1	1	6	1	9	3	6	3	6	2
Any of the above	6	6	31	24	28	24	20	14	23	18

Notes: All ages

Table 11.2 shows the number of times that injectors (those arrestees who had injected the drug) injected in the last 30 days. The table shows that the incidence of injection was highest among heroin injectors, who injected on average 20 days out of the last 30 days. Methadone and cocaine injectors did so on average just under once every other day (14 days out of the last 30). Injectors of amphetamines and other drugs did so at the lower rate of 12 days and 10 days out of the last 30 days respectively. The table also shows the percentage of high-rate injectors (injected 15 days or more in the last 30 days) in each group. Almost two-thirds (64%) of injectors of heroin were classified as high-rate injectors. About half of both methadone injectors (50%) and cocaine injectors (48%) were high-rate injectors.

Table 11.2: Mean number of days injected in the last 30 days

Period	Mean number of days injected in the last 30 days among injectors	Percentage of high rate injectors (used 15 days or more in the last 30 days) among injectors	Number of injectors in the last 30 days
Heroin	20.4	64	90
Methadone	13.7	50	6
Cocaine	13.7	48	42
Amphetamines	11.6	36	42
Other drug	10.0	29	7

Note: Among injectors of the specific drug type only in the last 30 days.

The next table draws on the findings of the repeat surveys in Nottingham and Sunderland. The prevalence of injection of any drug increased in both locations over the period 1997 to 1999. In Nottingham, 14 per cent of arrestees were found to have injected one or more drugs in the last 12 months in the 1997 survey, compared with 24 per cent in the 1999 survey. In Sunderland, 9 per cent of arrestees were found to have injected one or more drugs in the 1997 survey, compared with 14 per cent in the 1999 survey. The increase in Nottingham was statistically significant at a probability of p<.05 (the difference could have occurred by chance less than five times out of 100) and the increase in Sunderland was significant at a reduced level of probability of p<.13 (the difference could have occurred by chance less that 13 times out of 100).

The patterns of increase in injection across the two sites is consistent with the pattern of increase in prevalence of drug use across the two sites. In Nottingham, there was some evidence of an increase in both heroin and cocaine use (see Chapters 4 and 5). There is also some evidence of an increase in the prevalence of injection of these drugs. The prevalence of injecting heroin increased from eight per cent in 1997 to 16 per cent in 1999 and the prevalence of injecting cocaine increased from four per cent to six per cent (only the former change was statistically significant). In Sunderland, there was some evidence of an increase in both heroin and amphetamine use. In this site, the prevalence of injecting heroin increased from four per cent to seven per cent over the two surveys and the prevalence of injecting amphetamines increased from six per cent to eight per cent (neither finding was statistically significant). Hence, there is some evidence (not always supported by the significance tests) that changes in the prevalence of use of particular drugs might be associated with changes in the prevalence of injecting those drugs.

Table 11.3 : Percentage of all arrestees who reported injecting selected drugs in the last 12 months over time: 1997 and 1999

	Nottingham			Sunderland		
	1997	1999	Significance of difference	1997	1999	Significance of difference
	n=209	n=204		n=271	n=182	
Heroin	8	16	* (+)	4	7	ns
Methadone	3	0	ns	1	0	ns
Cocaine	4	6	ns	1	1	ns
Amphetamines	12	12	ns	6	8	ns
Other drug	3	3	ns	3	3	ns
Any of the above	14	24	* (+)	9	14	ns

Notes: *= p<.05; **= p<.01; ***=p<.001 Chi-squared test: corrected for 2X2 tables, where appropriate. (+) and (-) show the direction of change.

Table 11.4 examines the extent to which injectors shared their needles. In the developmental stage of the research, arrestees were asked simply whether they had ever shared their syringes or needles and whether they had done so in the last 12 months, without any further explanation. In more recent surveys, the interviewers have explained to the arrestee that sharing means using someone else's equipment, which had already been used, or someone using yours, regardless of whether you were both present at the time. It is possible that the absence of this qualification might have served to reduce the overall stated prevalence of sharing. Nevertheless, the results are reported below.

Overall, six per cent of all arrestees interviewed said that they had shared a needle at some time in their lives and four per cent said that they had done so in the last 12 months. The table also shows the results relating just to those arrestees who reported injecting drugs. Over a quarter (28%) of arrestees who had injected drugs in their lives had shared their equipment and one-fifth (20%) of arrestees who had injected in the last 12 months had shared their needles.

Table 11.4: Percentage of arrestees who reported sharing needles in their lifetime and during the last 12 months

	Shared ever		Shared in the last 12 months	
number all	n=740		n=740	
number injected	n=167		n=134	
	n	%	n	%
All arrestees who shared	46	6	27	4
Injectors who shared	46	28	27	20

These results show that a notable minority of all 'major' drug users injects the drugs and some of these injectors share needles. There is some evidence to support the view that as the prevalence of drug use increases the prevalence of problem behaviour relating to it (such as injection and sharing) increases. The increases in injecting shown for Nottingham and Sunderland also provide evidence of a connection. However, it is also likely that there are other factors that affect the willingness of users to inject, including cultural and sub-cultural differences and changes in fashion in methods of administering drugs. Nevertheless, the reported rates of injection and sharing in the current sample suggest that these are potential problems associated with drug misuse which might need to be tackled in their own right.

12   Treatment

One of the central platforms of the government's drugs strategy is tackling drug misuse through treatment provision. In order to be effective, the strategy needs to encourage users, who have not sought treatment, to do so. However, it also needs to satisfy the unmet demand for treatment among users who would like treatment, but, for one reason or another, have not received it.

The extent of the unmet need for treatment among drug users is largely unknown. In the current surveys, arrestees were asked whether they had ever been in treatment and whether they currently wanted treatment. Table 12.1 shows that about one-fifth (21%) of all arrestees had received treatment for drug misuse at some time in their lives and just over one-quarter (29%) said that they currently had a need for treatment. Of those who said that they currently needed treatment, about one-third of them (9% of the total sample) said that they were receiving treatment and two-thirds of them (20% of the total sample) said that they were not currently receiving treatment. Hence, about one-fifth (20%) of arrestees had an unmet need for treatment.

It is possible to use the results of the Nottingham and Sunderland repeat surveys to determine whether the use of treatment facilities among arrestees had changed over time. Table 12.2 shows that there has been little change in either area in the use of treatment facilities when comparing the 1997 survey with the 1999 survey. It will be possible to continue to monitor use of treatment facilities in later surveys to determine whether the proportion of drug-misusing arrestees using treatment facilities has increased over time.

Table 12.1:   Treatment received and wanted for drug use

Percentages

	South Norwood n=145	Liverpool n=209	Nottingham n=204	Sunderland n=182	All arrestees n=740
Treatment ever	15	34	21	11	21
Treatment wanted (currently received)	7	16	8	2	9
Treatment wanted (not currently received)	11	29	21	15	20

Table 12.2:   Treatment received for drug use in the past over time 1997 and 1999

	Nottingham			Sunderland		
	1997 n=209	1999 n=204	Significance of difference	1997 n=271	1999 n=182	Significance of difference
Yes	21	21	ns	13	11	ns
No	79	79		87	87	
Total	100	100		100	100	

Notes: *= p<.05; **= p<.01; ***=p<.001 Chi-squared test: corrected for 2X2 tables, where appropriate. (+) and (-) show the direction of change.

One of the key components of the success of the government's treatment strategy is provision of the kinds of treatment that arrestees want. Tables 12.3 and 12.4 show the nature and source of treatment services used by arrestees in the past and wanted in the future. The most common types of treatment ever received were evenly split between detoxification/withdrawal programmes and maintenance/ stabilisation programmes. The most common sources of treatment in the past were drugs clinics and general practitioners. A similar pattern emerges in relation to the nature and source of current treatment received. Perhaps the most important findings relate to those arrestees who have an unmet need for treatment. The most common kind of treatment wanted among this group was detoxification/withdrawal, mentioned by 10 per cent of all arrestees as a current treatment need. A further nine per cent said that they wanted individual counselling in relation to drug misuse and four per cent said that they wanted maintenance prescribing. The most commonly mentioned source of treatment wanted was from a drug clinic followed by a general practitioner.

Table 12.3:   Kinds of treatment received and wanted for drug use

Percentages

	Treatment ever	Treatment current [1]	Treatment wanted (none current) [2]
Detoxification/withdrawal	9	3	10
Maintenance/stabilisation	8	5	4
Counselling	6	2	9
Therapy individual	2	-	3
Therapy group	2	-	2
Self help	2	1	2
Other treatment	2	1	2

Notes: [1] Percentage calculated on the total number of all arrestees. [2] Percentages calculated on the number of arrestees not currently in treatment. '-'=less than 0.5%. Multiple responses possible.

Table 12.4:   Source of treatment received and wanted for drug use

Percentages

	Treatment ever	Treatment current	Treatment wanted (none current)
Drug clinic	9	4	8
General practitioner	7	4	6
Private practitioner	1	-	3
Hospital in-patient	2	0	4
Other residential	2	1	0
Other	3	1	3

Notes: [1] Percentage calculated on the total number of all arrestees. [2] Percentages calculated on the number of arrestees not currently in treatment. '-' = less than 0.5%. Multiple responses possible.

The results suggest that there is a substantial unmet need for treatment services among drug misusing arrestees. Their treatment needs are fairly mixed, combining programmes that will get them off drugs with programmes that will make their drug misuse safer and better controlled. The preferred source of drug treatment is also fairly mixed, with the strongest preferences for drugs clinics or general practitioners. However, other sources of treatment are also mentioned. Hence, the results suggest that in order for the treatment arm of the drugs strategy to be effective, it is necessary not only to provide additional treatment services, but also to provide the kinds of treatment services that are wanted and will be used.

In the second Sunderland survey, some additional questions were asked relating to the development of 'arrest referral schemes'. This was the most recent survey of the four reported in this publication and the questions were not included in the earlier surveys.

Arrestees were first asked whether they had been offered any kind of help or information relating to drug misuse during the last 12 months when in police custody. The results are shown in Table 12.5. Two per cent of arrestees arrested locally (within 5 miles from the current custody suite) and six per cent of those arrested out of the local area had received help or information about drugs while in police custody. In most cases (i.e. in relation to 6 of the 8 arrestees involved), the help or information offered was not followed up.

Table 12.5: **Whether help or information was offered on drug or alcohol use during police custody relating to previous arrests**

1999

Among arrestees reporting at least one previous arrest in the last 12 months: n=109

		Within 5 miles current custody suite		5 miles or further from current custody suite	
		n	%	n	%
Whether help or information was offered in the last12 months	Yes	2	2	6	6
	No	107	98	103	98
	Total	109	100	109	100
Whether help or information offered was followed up n=8	Yes	2	100	0	0
	No	0	0	6	100
	Total	2	100	6	100

Arrestees were asked about the nature of the help or information offered (see Table 12.6). In most cases, the help or information was individual counselling or information leaflets. Only one of the arrestees said that the help included referral to another agency or body outside of the police station. Three arrestees found the help or information useful and four found it not useful (one value was missing).

Table 12.6   ***Nature and usefulness of help or information offered on drug or alcohol use during police custody relating to previous arrests***

		n=7	% (of n=7)
Type of help or information offered [1]	Counselling	3	43
	Leaflets	3	43
	Referral	1	14
	General	1	14
Usefulness of help or information offered	Very useful	1	14
	Fairly useful	2	29
	Not very useful	1	14
	Not at all useful	3	43
	Total	7	100

[1] Multiple responses possible. Table includes only arrestees offered help or information: n=8. One missing value.

It should be noted that the idea of arrest referral was fairly new at the time of the Sunderland survey and there were very few schemes or related provisions in existence. Hence, the number of positive responses was low. However, the current findings might be regarded as baseline data on the state of arrest referral schemes and related programmes at about a time when the emphasis was to some extent focused on providing information. Future NEW-ADAM surveys will be able to monitor these developments and to measure the spread and nature of provision over time.

Conclusion on health and treatment

The third aim of current government drugs policy is to tackle some of the health problems associated with drug misuse. In particular, it aims to reduce use of drugs through the provision of treatment services and to reduce some of the harm associated with drug misuse by reducing the proportion of users who inject and the proportion of injectors who share.

The preceding section has considered some of the health and treatment issues relating to currently active offenders. The chapter on health and dependence showed that about one-third of all arrestees were currently dependent on at least one drug. In some areas, the figure was closer to half. In addition to dependence, arrestees also suffered a number of health problems ranging from simple infections to chronic diseases, including (very occasionally) hepatitis and AIDS.

The chapter on injecting drugs showed that about a quarter of all arrestees had injected an illegal drug at some time in their lives and about 20 per cent had done so in the last 12 months. Heroin users were more likely than other users to inject their drugs and to do so at a higher daily rate. There was some evidence of an increase over time in the prevalence of injection among heroin users in one of two sites investigated. About one-fifth of arrestees who injected a drug in the last 12 months shared the equipment.

The chapter on treatment needs showed that about 20 per cent of all arrestees said that they currently wanted treatment, but were not receiving treatment (the unmet need for treatment). Treatment needs varied among arrestees with some preference shown for drug clinic or general practitioner withdrawal or maintenance programmes. There was little evidence at the time of the survey of arrest referral schemes. Arrestees who had experienced arrest referral were divided in their views about its overall usefulness.

Part Four: Drug availability and drug markets

Key Performance Target Four

The fourth key target of the government's drugs stategy is to reduce access to all drugs amongst young people and to reduce access to heroin and cocaine in particular.

Local availability of drugs

The fourth key target focusses on drugs seizures and international policy and as such has a less direct link with the NEW-ADAM programme than the previous objectives. However, the surveys discussed in this report included a range of questions on drugs markets and the ease with which drugs could be obtained on the streets, which do have a bearing on the programme. Before discussing these findings, it is worth discussing briefly what is known from the research literature about local drug markets and the effectiveness of programmes which aim to disrupt local drug distribution.

Drug markets

The study by Edmunds et al. (1996) of drugs markets in London made an important contribution to conceptualising and identifying local drug markets. The research was based on six drug markets in London identified by local police and drug workers and by selected drug users who had purchased drugs on the streets. The researchers on the project conducted 191 interviews and site visits were conducted at each market location.

Eighty per cent of the users interviewed said that they had made their last purchase in an open or semi-open market. The majority (61%) said that they used more than one market. Most of them had a regular seller and the majority of these said that they could obtain credit from their seller. Three-quarters of the users contacted their sellers by telephone. They typically purchased heroin at £10 a bag and crack at £20 a rock. The average weekly expenditure on drugs was just over £400 among users who used both crack and heroin, just under £400 among crack users who did not use heroin, about £250 among heroin users who did not use crack, and about £150 for those who only used other drugs.

Tackling drug markets

Drug markets have tended to be tackled using low-level police enforcement strategies. These typically involve police crackdowns, target police patrols, 'hot spot' patrols or covert operations. However, other policing strategies such as problem-oriented policing and community-oriented policing have also been used to tackle street drug sales.

Sherman (1990) reviewed the results of 18 evaluations conducted in the United States on the effectiveness of police crackdowns. Seven of the 18 evaluations comprised crackdowns of open-air drug markets. The methods used by the police included police trailer crackdowns (Georgetown), police presence crackdowns (Lynn and Lawrence, Massachusetts), Operation Pressure Point (Lower-East Side, New York), Washington Square crackdown (New York), Operation Clean Sweep (Washington, D.C.), and citizen patrol crackdowns (Washington, D.C.). In six of the seven evaluations there was an initial (short-term) deterrent effect on drug sales following police action and in two of the seven studies there was evidence of a residual (longer-term) deterrent effect.

An evaluation of problem-oriented policing in St. Louis, Missouri, in the United States, examined the effectiveness of police attempts to disrupt local drug markets (Hope, 1994). A large number of calls for service to the police in one particular neighbourhood concerned a single address, which was the location of a street drug market. The address had resulted in over 100 calls for service within a six-month period. The police convened a meeting of property owners in the area and discussed various actions to be taken. One of the actions taken was to persuade the landlord of the problem address to sell the property. At the point of sale, the police helped evict the existing tenants. An analysis of calls for service over the programme period showed a reduction in calls from residents associated with the problem address. However, calls relating to drug problems in other addresses in the area increased.

There are fewer examples of evaluations of targeted policing strategies in England. Dorn et al. (1992) helped to bridge this gap by providing a useful compilation of examples of drug market enforcement strategies in Britain and America. The strategies discussed included 'buy and bust' operations, raids, sweeps, targeted policing and inconvenience policing. The descriptions of the case studies showed that some of the strategies had short-term effects on drug dealing through incapacitation (as a result of arrests) and deterrence (as a result of police presence).

Ease of access to drugs by arrestees

The research findings suggest that drug markets (both open and closed) are an important source of supply to drug users and that attempts to disrupt such markets might help to reduce the overall supply of drugs (at least in the short term). There is relatively little research on drugs markets in England and Wales and it is difficult to know how easy or difficult it is for users to purchase drugs should they wish to do so. The current section includes two chapters which address issues relating to drugs supply and drugs markets. The first chapter covers methods by which arrestees obtain heroin and crack/cocaine and the nature of the markets in which the drugs are purchased. The second chapter covers the issue of weapons and guns and the role that they play in committing crime and in making drug purchases.

13   Drug markets

One of the important factors that affects the level of drug use is local availability. If there are few drugs available in a local area, then at least some of the potential purchasers of these drugs will be unable to obtain them. The same argument applies to the ease of making the purchase. If it is difficult to make a purchase locally because the drugs are sold through fairly inaccessible closed markets, then some of the potential purchasers of these drugs will be unable to obtain them. There are a number of ways of measuring local availability and ease of obtaining drugs. The following two tables (Tables 13.1 and 13.2) list some of the factors that can determine whether drugs are available and easy to obtain.

The first table shows that, at the time of the survey, over 80 per cent of arrestees were able to obtain either crack/cocaine (82%) or heroin (85%) in their local neighbourhood. In other words, it was not necessary for them to travel beyond their local neighbourhood to obtain their drugs. The majority of arrestees (75% of crack/cocaine users and 79% of heroin users) made the initial contact by telephone (including mobile phones) or pager.

About one-third of arrestees (34% of crack/cocaine users and 29% of heroin users) had their drugs delivered to their door, while the remainder went somewhere to collect them. Those who went somewhere to collect them typically met someone on the street (59% of crack/cocaine users and 60% of heroin users) or went to someone's house (21% of crack/cocaine users and 27% of heroin users). Those who met someone on the street typically conducted the purchase in a residential area rather than a city centre area. The average number of dealers known to arrestees was 12 in relation to crack/cocaine and 15 in relation to heroin. The average amount spent per purchase was £52 in relation to crack/cocaine and £79 in relation to heroin.

The second table shows changes in the street availability of crack/cocaine and heroin over time in Nottingham and Sunderland. In 1997, 50 per cent of arrestees in Nottingham said that they could buy crack/cocaine and 60 per cent said that they could buy heroin in their own neighbourhood. In 1999, 81 per cent of arrestees said that they could buy crack/cocaine locally and 83 per cent said that they could buy heroin locally. Both increases were statistically significant. There was no comparable change in Sunderland.

In Nottingham, the mean number of people from whom arrestees could buy crack/cocaine increased from 10.3 in 1997 to 13.4 in 1999. Similarly, the number of people from whom arrestees could buy heroin increased from 13.8 in 1997 to 18.5 in 1999. However, neither change was statistically significant. In Sunderland, there was almost no change in the mean number of known dealers of crack/cocaine and there was a non-significant reduction in the number of known dealers of heroin.

Table 13.1: Method of purchasing crack/cocaine or heroin in the last 12 months

		Crack or cocaine n=131 %	Heroin n=106 %
Do you usually buy in your local neighbourhood?	Yes	82	85
	No	18	15
	Total	100	100
How do you usually initiate contact?	Phone/pager	75	79
	Personal contact	25	21
	Total	100	100
How do you usually obtain the purchase?	Delivered to door	34	29
	Go somewhere to collect it	66	71
	Total	100	100
(If go somewhere) What kinds of places?	Inside someone's house	21	27
	At the door or window	3	3
	In an abandoned building	0	0
	Pubs or clubs	13	7
	On the street	59	60
	Other	4	3
	Total	100	100
(If go somewhere) What kinds of areas?	Residential areas	65	69
	City centre areas	11	6
	Back-street areas	21	25
	Other	3	0
	Total	100	100
How many people can you currently buy from?	Mean number	12	15
How much did you buy last purchase?	Mean amount £s	£52	£79

Note: This question was included on the follow-up questionnaire, which was answered by half the sample. In addition, questions about crack/cocaine use and heroin use were answered only by arrestees who had used these drugs in the last 12 months. The number of arrestees allocated to follow-up questionnaire version 'B' was 360. The number of arrestees who answered questionnaire version B and had also consumed crack/cocaine was 131 and the number who had also consumed heroin was 106. Percentage calculated on valid cases only.

Table 13.2: Method of purchasing crack/cocaine or heroin in the last 12 months over time: 1997 and 1999

	Nottingham			Sunderland		
	1997	1999	Significance of difference	1997	1999	Significance of difference
	n=209	n=102		n=271	n=82	
Usually buy in neighbourhood	%	%		%	%	
Crack/cocaine	n=58	n=34		n=44	n=18	
Yes	50	81	* (+)	58	58	ns
No	50	19		42	42	
Total	100	100		100	100	
Heroin	n=50	n=35		n=28	n=18	
Yes	60	83	* (+)	77	77	ns
No	40	17		23	23	
Total	100	100		100	100	
Number of people buy from	n	n		n	n	
Crack/cocaine	n=58	n=34		n=44	n=18	
Mean number	10.3	13.4	ns	7.5	7.8	ns
Heroin	n=50	n=34		n=28	n=18	
Mean number	13.8	18.5	ns	18.4	8.6	ns

Notes: * = p<.05; ** = p<.01; *** = p<.001 Chi-squared test: corrected for 2X2 tables, where appropriate. (+) and (-) show the direction of change. Percentages and means calculated on valid cases only. In 1997, all arrestees were asked these questions. In 1999, only those arrestees allocated to follow-up questionnaire version 'B' were asked these questions. These questions also were answered only by arrestees who had consumed crack/cocaine or heroin in the last 12 months.

The changes in availability of drugs as measured through the ability to make local purchases and the number of dealers known to the user to some extent mirror the changes in the pattern of drug use in the two areas. In Nottingham, there was a significant increase across the two surveys in the proportion of arrestees involved in crack/cocaine and heroin use and a significant increase in the local availability of these drugs. In Sunderland, there was no significant increase in the use of these drugs among arrestees and there was no significant change in the availability of these drugs.

14   Weapons and guns

The possession and ownership of weapons and guns is problematic in a general sense, and legislation has recently been passed to tackle this problem by controlling the spread of both legal and illegal firearm possession. The use of weapons and guns in crime is even more problematic as the chance of injury or even death increases considerably. The use of weapons and guns in relation to drug use and drug purchases is also problematic as it increases the harm associated with drug use to include the possibility of injury or death. The combination of all three (drugs, crime and guns) is clearly of special concern.

A random sub-group of all arrestees were asked about ownership and access to weapons and guns. Some of the key findings are summarised in Table 14.1. About a quarter of arrestees (27%) said that they had carried a weapon (other than a gun) at the time of an offence at some time in their lives. Fifteen per cent said that they had carried a weapon at the time of an offence in the last 12 months. About one-third (36%) of arrestees said that they had owned or had easy access to a gun at some time in their lives and about one-quarter (24%) said that they had done so in the last 12 months. About a third of arrestees (30%) had mixed with people who owned or had access to a gun in the last 12 months.

It is not necessarily the case that the guns owned were illegal or that the firearms involved could be used in connection with a crime. In fact, 9 per cent of arrestees said that they had recently owned or had easy access to a gun for the purposes of hunting or target shooting and one per cent said that they owned or had easy access to a gun as part of their legitimate job. However, 13 per cent of arrestees said that they had recently owned or had easy access to a gun for protection or self defence, three per cent said that they had a gun for use in criminal activity and one per cent said that they had a gun to impress people. The type of guns owned or to which they had easy access were more frequently hand guns/pistols or shotguns.

Table 14.1: Access to and use of weapons and guns ever and in the last 12 months

Percentages

		Ever n=380	In the last 12 months n=380
Have you had a weapon (apart from a gun) on you when committing an offence?	Yes, a knife	14	8
	Yes, another weapon	9	5
	Yes, both	4	2
	No	73	85
	Total	100	100
Have your ever owned or had easy access to a gun?	Yes, owned and/or had easy access to a gun	36	24
	No, neither own nor had easy access to a gun	64	76
	Total	100	100
Have you ever mixed with people who owned or had easy access to a gun?	Yes, people mixed with owned or had easy access to a gun	36	30
	No, people mixed with did not own or have easy access to a gun	64	70
	Total	100	100
What kind of gun have you owned or had easy access to? [1]	Air gun/rifle	12	8
	Handgun pistol	18	12
	Shotgun	15	11
	Rifle	5	5
	Other gun	5	3
	Not sure what type	2	1
What were your reasons for owning or having easy access to a gun? [1]	Hunting/target shooting	12	9
	Protection/self-defence	16	13
	Use in criminal activity	5	3
	As a legitimate part of job	2	1
	To impress people	2	1
	Other	6	4
Have your ever had a gun with you when committing an offence? [1]	Yes	5	3

Note: This question was included on the follow-up questionnaire, which was answered by half the sample. The number of arrestees allocated to follow-up questionnaire version 'A' was 380. Percentages calculated on valid cases only. [1] These questions were put only to those arrestees who said that they had owned or had access to a gun. Multiple responses possible in relation to the questions on type of gun.

Table 14.2 shows some of the same results broken down by area (not all of the questions were asked in each of the four areas). The table shows little variation across the four sites in terms of use of weapons other than guns in crime. About 10 per cent to 20 per cent of arrestees in each site said that they had used a knife or other (non-gun) weapon in a crime in the last 12 months. There was also little variation across sites in terms of ownership or access to guns. About 20 per cent to 30 per cent of arrestees said that they had owned or had access to a gun in the last 12 months. The highest prevalence rate of gun ownership and access was in South Norwood (29%) and the lowest rate was in Nottingham (20%).

Table 14.2 : Access to and use of weapons and guns in the last 12 months by area

Percentages

		South Norwood n=73	Liverpool n=108	Nottingham n=102	Sunderland n=97
Have you had a weapon (apart from a gun) on you when committing an offence? [1]					
	Yes, a knife	7	7	7	12
	Yes, another weapon	7	3	5	7
	Yes, both	1	3	1	1
	No	85	88	87	80
	Total	100	100	100	100
Have your ever owned or had easy access to a gun?					
	Yes, owned and/or had easy access to a gun	29	22	20	27
	No, neither own nor had easy access to a gun	71	78	80	73
	Total	100	100	100	100

Note: This question was included on the follow-up questionnaire, which was answered by half the sample. The number of arrestees allocated to follow-up questionnaire version 'A' was 380. Percentages calculated on valid cases only. [1] These questions were put only to those arrestees who said that they had owned or had access to a gun. Multiple responses possible in relation to the questions on type of gun.

The final table in this chapter shows trends in gun ownership and access among arrestees over time. In Nottingham, there was a small (non-significant) increase in gun ownership and access during the period 1997 to 1999 (increasing from 16% to 20%). There was no change in the proportion of arrestees who said that they mixed with people who owned or had easy access to guns. In Sunderland, there was also a small and non-significant increase in gun ownership and easy access (23% to 27%), which was accompanied by a small reduction in the number of people mixed with who owned or had easy access to a gun.

Table 14.3: **Ownership and access to guns in the last 12 months over time: 1997 and 1999**

		Nottingham			Sunderland		
		1997	1999	Signif- cance of diff'	1997	1999	Signif- cance of diff'
		n=209	n=102		n=271	n=100	
Owned or had easy access to a gun?	Yes, owned and/or had easy access to a gun	16	20	ns	23	27	ns
	No, neither own nor had easy access to a gun	84	80		77	73	
	Total	100	100		100	100	
Mixed with people who owned or had easy access to a gun?	Yes, people mixed with owned or had easy access to a gun	38	38	ns	49	34	* (-)
	No, people mixed with did not own or have easy access to a gun	62	62		51	66	
	Total	100	100		100	100	

Notes: *= p<.05; **= p<.01; ***=p<.001 Chi-squared test: corrected for 2X2 tables, where appropriate. (+) and (-) show the direction of change. Percentages and means calculated on valid cases only. In 1997, all arrestees were asked these questions. In 1999, only those arrestees allocated to follow-up questionnaire version 'B' were asked these questions.

Overall, the chapter has shown what might be regarded as high levels of involvement of arrestees with guns and other weapons. There is some indication (not statistically significant) that gun ownership and easy access to guns may have increased slightly since 1997. However, this finding is very tentative and future NEW-ADAM surveys will help to monitor trends in gun ownership among criminally active offenders.

The chapter has also shown that not all arrestees who own or have easy access to guns do so illegally. Some own or have easy access to guns as a result of hunting or target shooting and some have legitimate access as part of their job. Hence, it might be useful to think in terms of two or more distinct groups of arrestees who own guns or have easy access to guns for different reasons. Some of them may use guns legitimately (or illegitimately) for hunting and target practice, while others may use guns as part of criminal activity and drug use. One important reason given for gun ownership or access among this latter group of arrestees was that a gun offered protection when buying or selling drugs.

Conclusion on drug availability and drug markets

The fourth aim of the government's drugs strategy is to reduce the availability of drugs on the streets, with particular reference to heroin and cocaine. The strategy relates mainly to national and international level enforcement and covers various issues beyond those of the NEW-ADAM programme. However, there are some results from the survey which are relevant to this aim.

The first chapter in this section showed that arrestees generally found it easy to obtain heroin and crack/cocaine on the streets. The majority were able to purchase these drugs in their own neighbourhood and about one-third of them had the drugs delivered to their door. Arrestees tended to know a large number of potential dealers and had little difficulty in obtaining their drugs. There was some evidence that it has become easier to obtain heroin and crack/cocaine since the first surveys in 1997.

The second chapter looks at weapons and guns. About one-quarter of arrestees said that they had carried a weapon with them at the time of an offence at some time in their lives and about one-third said that they had owned or had easy access to a gun. Some of the arrestees owned or had easy access to a gun for potentionally legitimate purposes such as hunting or target shooting. However, the majority said that they owned or had easy access to a gun for protection or self defence. One reason given for needing protection was at the time of buying or selling drugs.

15   Conclusion

The current report has presented the main findings from the second developmental stage of the NEW-ADAM programme and it has done so within the context of the four main strands of the government's drugs strategy. The main aims of the strategy were discussed in Chapter 1. The policy is based on routine monitoring of patterns and trends in drug use as a means of evaluating effectiveness and, as such, is similar to other prevention-oriented strategies (e.g. policing and crime prevention) to the extent that is knowledge-based. It is perhaps appropriate, therefore, in this concluding chapter, to reflect briefly on what is now known about patterns and trends in drug misuse and to consider the contribution of the NEW-ADAM programme and ADAM programmes in other countries to this developing knowledge base.

Other UK research

Drugs research in the UK has made some important advances in the last few years. The drugs component of the British Crime Survey has been included in the last three surveys and is set to continue as part of the regular monitoring of drug misuse within the general population. The results of the survey are particularly important in identifying trends in drug misuse over time and in monitoring the uneven distribution of drug misuse across the country. The most recent findings have indicated an increase in cocaine use over the last two years, reflecting to some extent the increases shown in the current NEW-ADAM report.

The schools surveys conducted by the Schools Health Education Unit in Exeter and the Government plan to conduct schools surveys among representative samples of schools throughout England and Wales will help monitor drug use patterns and trends among younger members of the general population not covered by general household surveys. The recent decline in prevalence in drug use among school-age children noted in both the Balding (2000) and Plant and Miller (2000) studies is interesting and worth monitoring further along with any implication that the trend might have for drug use among post-school age young people.

Official statistics have also helped to build up a picture of drug misuse. Data on drug seizures and offenders processed for drug offences each indicate recent rises in drug use generally and in heroin and crack/cocaine use in particular. The results of the regular analyses of the Regional Drug Misuse Databases have also added to the picture of drug misuse and confirm recent increases in the most dangerous forms of drug misuse identified in the other data sources. It is expected that the RDMD will be developed further over the forthcoming years and will provide an important addition to the drug misuse knowledge base.

The ADAM programme

The ADAM programme publishes data on drug misuse among arrestees in the United States and, as such, is not directly comparable with drug misuse in the UK. However, it is worth mentioning briefly some of the more recent findings of the ADAM programme and also the results of a comparison of drug misuse among arrestees in the US and England and Wales conducted using data from the first developmental stage of the NEW-ADAM programme.

The most recent ADAM report for 1998 provides information on drug use among arrestees in 35 communities in the United States (National Institute of Justice, 1999). Unlike the NEW-ADAM programme, the US programme is based on four surveys a year in each survey site. The trend analyses show quite clear patterns in drug use. Over the last five years (the period covered by the most recent report), the prevalence of arrestees testing positive for cocaine has gradually declined and, during the period 1997 to 1998, the percentage of positive tests for cocaine decreased in the majority of the survey sites. In New York City in the first quarter of 1995, for example, over three-quarters of male arrestees tested positive for cocaine. In the first quarter of 1998, the prevalence fell to below 60 per cent and by the last quarter of 1998, the prevalence was close to 40 per cent.

Over the same period of time, the prevalence of positive tests for opiates has remained low (by comparison with England). In only eight of the 35 ADAM sites in 1998 did more than 10 per cent of the adult males population test positive for opiates. The highest prevalence rates were in Philadelphia and Chicago in which 18 per cent of adult males in each area tested positive for opiates. However, there is some evidence of a slight increase over time in the prevalence of positive tests for opiate use in some sites (e.g. in Detroit, New Orleans, and Philadelphia).

It is too early to tell whether these developments represent the beginning of a reversal in recent trends which have resulted in the US arrestees having higher cocaine use rates and lower heroin use rates than Britain.

The results of the ADAM programme and the NEW-ADAM programme were brought together in a comparison report based on data from surveys conducted in the respective countries in 1996-97 (based on the results of the first developmental stage of the NEW-ADAM programme)(Taylor and Bennett, 1999). The data were matched in various ways to improve their comparability, including using matched sites, using the same cut-off levels for the urinalysis, and weighting the samples on various demographic criteria.

The results of the urinalysis showed that the prevalence rates of positive tests were higher in England than the United States for four of the six drug types compared (marijuana, opiates, methadone and amphetamines). There was no significant difference across the two countries in the prevalence of positive tests for benzodiazepines. The prevalence of positive tests for cocaine was significantly higher in the United States than in England. The report made some tentative steps in explaining the difference in patterns of drug use among arrestees across the two countries. One possible explanation concerns the nature of supply factors, including the location of the United States and Britain in relation to the dominant drug trade routes. Another possible explanation concerns the nature of demand factors, including cultural differences between the two countries. However, the nature of the differences and the explanations of the differences require additional analysis and it is hoped that further comparisons will be made as part of developments in the I-ADAM programme.

The I-ADAM programme

It was mentioned earlier that a consortium had recently been established of countries currently active in conducting research based on interviewing and drug-testing arrestees. The consortium is known as the I-ADAM programme and currently includes eight active members (Australia, Chile, England, Malaysia, The Netherlands, Scotland, South Africa and Taiwan). The programme is still very new and only a small number of countries have conducted surveys and generated findings. However, it might be worth summarising briefly what these countries have found to date.

Australia has been active in developing the framework of its DUMA (Drug Use Monitoring in Australia) programme. DUMA is described as a pilot project that seeks to measure drug use amongst those people who have been charged with a criminal offence (Makkai, 1999). It describes its aims as improving the quality of data available on illicit drug use in the offender population, providing an early warning system for changes in patterns of illicit drug use, and establishing a mechanism whereby local and national enforcement can evaluate policy initiatives.

The early results of surveys conducted in New South Wales (in the local area police commands at Bankstown and Parramatta) have recently been published (Makkai, Fitzgerald and Doak, 2000). The findings are based on two surveys in each site conducted in the summer and autumn quarters of 1999 involving a total of 379 completed interviews. Fifty-six per cent of arrestees interview provided a urine sample. The interviewees ranged in age from 10 to over 50. The results of the urinalysis showed that 53 per cent tested positive for cannabis (compared with 49% shown earlier as part of the second developmental stage of the NEW-ADAM programme). Forty-three per cent tested positive for heroin (compared with 29% for opiates in the NEW-ADAM surveys) and two per cent tested positive for cocaine (compared with 20% for crack/cocaine in the NEW-ADAM surveys).

Early results are also available from research conducted in South Africa by the researchers from the Medical Research Council and the Institute for Security Studies (Parry, 1999). The pilot study, called the 3-Metros Arrestee Study, was based in nine police stations in Gauteng, Cape Town and Durban and involved interviews with 970 arrestees. Ninety per cent of arrestees agreed to give a urine specimen. The surveys were conducted in August and September in 1999 and further surveys are planned for 2000. The results showed that nearly half (49%) of arrestees tested positive for one or more drugs. Twenty-five per cent tested positive for mandrax, two per cent tested positive for opiates, and four per cent tested positive for cocaine.

A pilot programme of interviewing and drug testing of arrestees in Scotland has recently been completed and a report has been produced. The research has been conducted by a consortium of researchers at the University of Glasgow, including the Centre for Drug Misuse Research. However, at the time of writing the results are only just being published (McKeganey et al. 2000). The results will be of obvious importance both in their own right and in providing a comparison with England and Wales.

A pilot survey of arrestees has also been conducted (during the summer, 1999) in the Hague, in The Netherlands. The survey was funded by the Ministry of Justice, Directorate of Strategic Planning. The results of the survey have not yet been published. Arrestee surveys have also been conducted in police stations in Santiago, Chile (results not yet published) and surveys are planned in Taiwan and Penang in Malaysia.

Clearly, the I-ADAM programme is at an early stage in its developments and most countries (with the exception of the United States and England and Wales) are still in the developmental stages of the research. Once established, however, the I-ADAM research consortium will be a potent force in monitoring and analysing patterns and trends in drug misuse, both nationally and internationally. It is envisioned that participating countries will develop an integrated data base comprising a core set of variables generated by identical procedures, plus additional country-specific variables.

The NEW-ADAM programme

The NEW-ADAM programme was formally established in July 1999, as mentioned in the first chapter of the report. The first round of funding for the programme covers three financial years beginning 1999–2000 and ending 2001–2002. In each financial year (including the foreshortened first year), eight surveys will be completed in eight different locations. In the first and second years a total of 16 different sites (8 per year) will be selected and surveyed. In the third year, the eight sites selected in the first year will be returned to and repeat surveys will be conducted. Should funding continue beyond the first three years, the research would continue this pattern and in the fourth year the eight sites surveyed in the second year would be returned to, and so on. The programme would generate both cross-sectional and longitudinal data of drug misuse among arrestees in selected sites across England and Wales and over time. It is hoped that the programme will play a role in monitoring patterns and trends in drug use among currently active offenders and, in so doing, will help fill a gap in our knowledge about drug misuse and its links with crime.

Appendix A: Survey details

Table A3.1: Total arrestees eligible and ineligible to be approached for interview

	n	%
Total arrestees processed during the period of the research	2,971	100
Eligible	1,401	47
Ineligible	1,570	53
Total	2,971	100

Table A3.2: Reasons for ineligibility

	n	%
Total ineligible	1,570	100
Unfit due to alcohol intoxication	460	29
Unfit due to drugs intoxication	25	2
Mentally disordered	269	17
Children/juveniles	247	16
Required interpreter	48	3
Potentially violent	63	4
In custody for more than 48 hours	39	3
At discretion of staff	63	4
Drink driving/drunkenness	40	3
Other/unknown	316	20
Total	1,570	100

Table A3.3: Total eligible arrestees approached for interview

	n	%
Total eligible arrestees	1,401	100
Approached	911	65
Not approached	490	35
Total	1,401	100

Table A3.4: **Reasons for non approach**

	n	%
Total not approached	490	100
No custody staff available	9	2
Researcher with another arrestee at the time	92	19
No researcher on duty at the time	10	2
Researcher unavailable at the time	8	2
Time in custody too short	260	53
Other/unknown	111	23
Total	490	100

Table A3.5: **Total arrestees approached who were interviewed**

	n	%
Total arrestees approached	911	100
Interviewed	740	81
Not interviewed	171	19
Total	911	100

Table A3.6: **Reasons for non interview**

	n	%
Total not interviewed	171	100
Refused	106	62
Other/unknown	65	38
Total	171	100

Table A3.7: **Total arrestees interviewed who gave a urine specimen**

	n	%
Total arrestees interviewed	740	100
Specimen	506	68
No specimen	234	32
Total	740	100

Table A3.8:   *Reasons for non specimen*

	n	%
Total no specimen	234	100
Agreed – unsuccessful	69	30
Refused	79	34
Other/unknown	86	37
Total	234	100

Appendix B: Supplementary tables

Table B3.1:   Achieved samples in Nottingham and Sunderland: 1997 and 1999

| | Nottingham | | | | Sunderland | | | |
| | 1997 | | 1999 | | 1997 | | 1999 | |
	n	% of previous row	n	% of previous row	n	% of previous row	n	% of previous row
Total arrestees processed	781	100	909	100	635	100	654	100
Arrestees eligible	406	52	420	46	397	63	255	39
Arrestees approached	246	61	244	58	311	78	216	85
Arrestees interviewed	209	85	204	84	271	87	182	84
Arrestees providing a urine specimen [3]	132	63	132	65	210	77	169	93

Table B3.2: Characteristics of the eligible population and achieved interview in Nottingham and Sunderland: 1997 and 1999

Percentages

		Nottingham				Sunderland			
		1997		1999		1997		1999	
		Sample n=209	Population n=406	Sample n=204	Population n=420	Sample n=271	Population n=397	Sample n=182	Population n=255
Sex	Male	79	74	83	77	87	86	86	85
	Female	21	26	17	23	13	14	14	15
	Total	100	100	100	100	100	100	100	100
Age	17–19	19	17	24	22	30	27	29	27
	20–24	32	31	31	30	26	25	20	20
	25–29	19	19	20	21	18	17	18	18
	30–59	31	32	25	26	26	30	34	35
	60 or over	0	1	0	1	0	1	0	1
	Total	100	100	100	100	100	100	100	100
Race	White	90	83	85	81	98	97	98	98
	Non-white	10	17	15	19	2	3	2	2
	Total	100	100	100	100	100	100	100	100

Notes: The population includes eligible cases only. Percentages calculated on valid cases only. It should be noted that the sample is based on unique arrestees (repeat arrestees are not included), whereas the population is based on arrest events (repeat arrestees are included). The table does not include significance tests as the comparison groups are not based on independent samples. In more recent surveys, it has been possible to identify repeat arrestees in the population and to calculate the characteristics of the sample and the population on the basis of unique individuals.

Table B4.1: *Percentage positive tests among arrestees held for common offence types*

	Cannabis	Opiates	Methadone	Cocaine	Amphetamines	Benzodiazepines	Alcohol	Any drug (excl. alcohol)	Multiple drugs (excl. alcohol)	Total arrestees held for specific offence
Assault	34	24	7	12	10	10	32	61	27	41
Wounding	40	20	0	20	0	0	0	60	20	5
Threats	25	0	0	0	0	0	25	25	0	4
Firearms/ weapons	60	20	40	0	0	0	40	80	40	5
Abduction/ kidnapping	33	33	0	33	0	0	0	33	33	3
Sex offences	0	0	0	0	0	0	0	0	0	2
Robbery	75	25	25	25	0	0	75	100	25	4
Burglary dwelling	56	20	4	8	16	24	8	76	32	25
Burglary non-dwelling	33	67	8	50	17	42	17	83	67	12
Theft person	0	0	0	0	0	0	0	0	0	1
Theft cycle	100	100	0	0	0	0	0	100	100	1
Theft from vehicle	50	0	0	0	0	0	0	50	0	2
Theft of/ taking vehicle	68	16	8	19	11	19	30	78	38	37
Theft shoplifting	60	64	33	41	17	26	7	86	74	42
Theft other	52	36	3	13	16	13	13	81	36	31
Handling	50	25	0	0	25	50	25	50	50	4
Fraud/ deception	20	20	0	20	20	0	0	40	20	5
Going equipped	75	50	25	75	0	25	0	100	75	4
Criminal damage	46	25	8	8	21	4	29	58	33	24

Table B4.1: **Percentage positive tests among arrestees held for common offence types (continued)**

	Cannabis	Opiates	Methadone	Cocaine	Amphetamines	Benzodiazepines	Alcohol	Any drug (excl. alcohol)	Multiple drugs (excl. alcohol)	Total arrestees held for specific offence
Drugs supply	75	38	0	25	0	13	13	88	25	8
Drugs possession	74	28	2	28	21	5	26	86	47	43
Drunkenness	17	17	0	0	0	0	67	33	0	6
Drink driving	0	0	0	0	0	0	100	0	0	2
POA Violent disorder	50	0	0	0	0	0	50	50	0	2
POA Affray	50	0	0	0	0	0	0	50	0	2
Breach of the peace	17	11	0	0	11	6	61	33	11	18
Disqualified driving	50	33	0	17	0	0	0	83	17	6
Prostitution related	100	100	0	100	0	0	0	100	100	1
Making off without payment	100	0	0	0	0	0	0	100	0	1

Notes: Includes only those arrestees who provided a specimen and were held for the offences shown. Arrestees held for more than one offence have been coded in terms of the most serious offence using the scale published by Phillips and Brown (1998). The percentages shown in the above table are sometimes based on very small numbers and should be treated with appropriate caution.

References

Balding, J. (1998) *Young People and Illegal Drugs in 1998.* Exeter: Schools Health Education Unit.

Balding, J. (2000) *Young People and Illegal Drugs in 2000.* Exeter: Schools Health Education Unit.

Bennett, T.H. (1991) 'Drug use and criminal behaviour'. In: I.B. Glass (ed.) *The International Handbook of Addiction Behaviour.* London: Routledge.

Bennett, T.H. (1995) *A Feasibility Study of Drug Testing of Arrestees in England and Wales.* Cambridge: Institute of Criminology.

Bennett, T.H. (1998) *Drugs and Crime: The Results of Research on Drug Testing and Interviewing Arrestees.* Home Office Research Study 183. London: Home Office.

Bennett, T.H. and Wright, R. (1986) 'The impact of prescribing on the crimes of opioid users', *British Journal of Addiction,* Vol.81, pp 307–315.

Brain, K., Parker, H. and Bottomley, T. (1998) *Evolving Crack Cocaine Careers: New Users, Quitters and Long Term Combination Drug Users in N.W. England.* Manchester: University of Manchester.

Collins, J.J., Hubbard, R.L., Rachal, J.V. (1985) 'Expensive drug use and illegal income: A Test of Explanatory Hypotheses', *Criminology,* Vol.23, No.4, pp 743–764.

Department of Health (1999) *Statistical Bulletin: Statistics from the Regional Drug Misuse Databases for Six Months Ending March 1999,* Issue 1999/33. London: Department of Health.

Dorn, N., Murji, K. and South, N. (1992) *Traffickers: Drug Markets and Law Enforcement.* London: Routledge.

Edgar, K. and O'Donnell, I. (1998) *Mandatory Drug Testing in Prisons: The Relationship Between MDT and the Level and Nature of Drug Misuse.* Home Office Research Study 189. London: Home Office.

Edmunds, M., Hough, M. and Urquia, (1996) *Tackling Local Drug Markets*. Crime Detection and Prevention Series Paper 80. Police Research Group. London: Home Office

Edmunds, M., Hough, M., Turnbull, P. and May, T. (1999) *Doing Justice to Treatment: Referring Offenders to Drug Services*. Drug Prevention Advisory Service Paper 2. London: Home Office.

Fendrich, M. and Yanchun, X. (1994) 'The validity of drug use reports from juvenile arrestees', *The International Journal of the Addictions*. Vol.29. pp 971–1985.

Gossop, M., Marsden, J. and Stewart, D. (1998) *NTORS at One Year: Changes in Substance Use, Health and Criminal Behaviour One Year after Intake*. London: Department of Health.

Graham, J. and Bowling, B. (1995) *Young People and Crime*. Home Office Research Study 145. London: Home Office.

Hammersley, R., Forsyth, A., Morrison, V., Davies, J.B. (1989) 'The relationship between crime and opioid use', *British Journal of Addiction*, Vol.84, pp 1029–1043.

HMG (Her Majesty's Government) (1998) *Tackling Drugs to Build a Better Britain*. London: Stationery Office.

Hope, T. (1994) 'Problem-oriented policing and drug-market locations: three case studies'. In: Clarke, R.V. *Crime Prevention Studies*, Vol.2. Munsby, NY: Criminal Justice Press.

Inciardi, J., McBride, D., McCoy, V. and Chitwood. D. (1994) 'Recent research on the crack/cocaine/crime connection', *Studies on Crime and Crime Prevention*, Vol.3, pp 63-79.

Jarvis, G., and Parker, H. (1989) 'Young heroin users and crime. How do the 'new users' finance their habits?', *British Journal of Criminology*. Vol.29, No.2, pp 175–185.

Leitner, M., Shapland, J. and Wiles, P. (1993) *Drug Usage and Drugs Prevention: The Views and Habits of the General Public*. London: HMSO.

Maden, A., Swinton, M. and Gunn, J. (1992) 'A survey of pre-arrest drug use in sentenced prisoners', *British Journal of Addiction*, Vol.87, pp.27-33.

Makkai, T. (1999) *Drug Use Monitoring in Australia (DUMA): A Brief Description.* Australian Institute of Criminology, Research and Public Policy Series No.21. Canberra: Australian Institute of Criminology.

Makkai, T., Fitzgerald, J. and Doak, P. (2000) *Drug use among Police Detainees.* Crime and Justice Bulletin. No.49. Sydney: NSW Bureau of Crime Statistics and Research.

McKeganey, N., Connelly, C., Knepil, J., Norrie, J., and Reid, L. (2000) *Interviewing and drug testing of arrestees in Scotland.* Glasgow: Centre for Drug Misuse.

National Institute of Justice (1999) 1998 *Annual Report on Drug Use Among Adult and Juvenile Arrestees.* Washington, D.C. U.S. Department of Justice.

Otero-Lopez, J.M., Martin, A.L., Miron-Redondon, L., Carrillo-De-La-Pena, M.T., Romero-Trinanes, E. (1994) 'An empirical study of the relationships between drug abuse and delinquency among adolescents', *British Journal of Criminology,* Vol.34, No. 4.

Parker, H., Measham, F. and Aldridge, J. (1995) *Drug Futures: changing Patterns of Drug use amongst English Youth.* London: ISDD.

Parker, H. and Kirby, P. (1996) *Methadone Maintenance and Crime Reduction on Merseyside.* Crime Detection and Prevention Series Paper 72. Police Research Group. London: Home Office.

Parker, H., Aldridge, J. and Measham, F. (1998) *Illegal Leisure: The Normalization of Adolescent Recreational Drug Use.* London Routledge.

Parry, C. (1999) *Press Release: Findings from a Groundbreaking Survey of Drug Use and Crime: The MRC/ISS 3-Metros Arrestee Study.* 6th December. Press release provided by the author.

Phillips, C. and Brown, D. (1998) *Entry into the Criminal Justice System: A Survey of Police Arrests and their Outcomes.* Home Office Research Study 185. London: Home Office.

Plant, M. and Miller, P. (2000) 'Drug use has declined among teenagers in United Kingdom'. *British Medical Journal.* Vol. 320, pp 1536.

Ramsay, M. and Percy, A. (1996) *Drug Misuse Declared: Results of the 1994 British Crime Survey.* Home Office Research Study 151. London: Home Office.

Ramsay, M. and Partridge, S. (1999) *Drug Misuse Declared in 1998: Results of the British Crime Survey.* Home Office Research Study 197. London: Home Office.

Ramsay, M. and Spiller, J. (1997) *Drug Misuse Declared in 1996: latest results from the British Crime Survey.* Home Office Research Study 172. London: Home Office.

Sherman, L. (1990) 'Police crackdowns: initial and residual deterrence.' In: M. Tonry and N. Morris (eds.) *Crime and Justice: A Review of Research, Vol.12.* Chicago: University of Chicago Press.

Taylor, B. and Bennett, T.H. (1999) *Comparing Drug Use Rates of Detained Arrestees in the United States and England.* National Institute of Justice, Washington, D.C.: U.S. Department of Justice.

UKADCU (United Kingdom Anti-Drugs Co-ordination Unit) (1999) *First Annual Report and National Plan.* London: Cabinet Office.

Wish, E.D. and Gropper, B.A. (1990) 'Drug testing by the criminal justice system: methods, research, and applications'. In: M. Tonry and J.Q. Wilson, *Drugs and Crime.* London: The University of Chicago Press.

RDS Publications

Requests for Publications

Copies of our publications and a list of those currently available may be obtained from:

Home Office
Research, Development and Statistics Directorate
Communications Development Unit
Room 201, Home Office
50 Queen Anne's Gate
London SW1H 9AT
Telephone: 020 7273 2084 (answerphone outside of office hours)
Facsimile: 020 7222 0211
E-mail: publications.rds@homeoffice.gsi.gov.uk

alternatively

why not visit the RDS web-site at
        Internet: http://www.homeoffice.gov.uk/rds/index.htm

where many of our publications are availabe to be read on screen or downloaded for printing.